Assessment Book

Scott Foresman
Science
The Diamond Edition

PEARSON
Scott Foresman

Editorial Offices: Glenview, Illinois • Parsippany, New Jersey • New York, New York
Sales Offices: Needham, Massachusetts • Duluth, Georgia • Glenview, Illinois
Coppell, Texas • Sacramento, California • Mesa, Arizona

www.sfsuccessnet.com

Series Authors

Dr. Timothy Cooney

Professor of Earth Science and Science Education
University of Northern Iowa (UNI)
Cedar Falls, Iowa

Dr. Jim Cummins

Professor
Department of Curriculum, Teaching, and Learning
The University of Toronto
Toronto, Canada

Dr. James Flood

Distinguished Professor of Literacy and Language
School of Teacher Education
San Diego State University
San Diego, California

Barbara Kay Foots, M.Ed.

Science Education Consultant
Houston, Texas

Dr. M. Jenice Goldston

Associate Professor of Science Education
Department of Elementary Education Programs
University of Alabama
Tuscaloosa, Alabama

Dr. Shirley Gholston Key

Associate Professor of Science Education
Instruction and Curriculum Leadership
Department College of Education
University of Memphis
Memphis, Tennessee

Dr. Diane Lapp

Distinguished Professor of Reading and Language Arts in Teacher Education
San Diego State University
San Diego, California

Sheryl A. Mercier

Classroom Teacher
Dunlap Elementary School
Dunlap, California

Dr. Karen L. Ostlund

Uteach Specialist
College of Natural Sciences
The University of Texas at Austin
Austin, Texas

Dr. Nancy Romance

Professor of Science Education & Principal Investigator
NSF/IERI Science IDEAS Project
Charles E. Schmidt College of Science
Florida Atlantic University
Boca Raton, Florida

Dr. William Tate

Chair and Professor of Education and Applied Statistics
Department of Education
Washington University
St. Louis, Missouri

Dr. Kathryn C. Thornton

Former NASA Astronaut Professor
School of Engineering and Applied Science
University of Virginia
Charlottesville, Virginia

Dr. Leon Ukens

Professor Emeritus
Department of Physics, Astronomy, and Geosciences
Towson University
Towson, Maryland

Steve Weinberg

Consultant
Connecticut Center for Advanced Technology
East Hartford, Connecticut

Consulting Author

Dr. Michael P. Klentschy

Superintendent
El Centro Elementary School District
El Centro, California

ISBN-13: 978-0-328-33394-3; ISBN-10: 0-328-33394-8

© Pearson Education, Inc.

Unit A
Life Science

Unit B
Earth Science

Unit C
Physical Science

Unit D
Space and Technology

Assessment Overview for the *Scott Foresman Science* Program

The *Scott Foresman Science* program provides a variety of assessment options in the Student Edition, Teacher's Edition, and Assessment Book.

Formal Assessment

Student Edition
- Chapter Review and Test Prep, with prescriptions for Intervention and Remediation in the Teacher's Edition
- Unit Test Talk (test-taking strategies)

Assessment Book
- Chapter Tests, with prescriptions for Intervention and Remediation
- Unit Tests
- Unit Test Talk (test-taking strategies)
- Unit Writing Prompts

ExamView
- Chapter Tests online or through ExamView CD-ROM

Ongoing Assessment

Student Edition
- Checkpoint questions for each lesson

Teacher's Edition
- Diagnostic check for each lesson
- Scaffolded Questions throughout lessons

Performance Assessment

Student Edition
- Unit Wrap-Up

Assessment Book
- Unit Performance Test

Assessment Book Overview

The Assessment Book is divided in two parts. The first part of the book provides assessment pages to photocopy for students. The second part of the book provides teacher support and answers.

Chapter and Unit Tests

The Chapter and Unit Tests assess students' understanding of science concepts and their ability to apply and analyze what they have learned. Tests include multiple-choice, short-response, and extended-response questions. The short-response questions (worth 2 points) and the extended-response questions (worth 4 points) involve analysis and application of knowledge. An Intervention and Remediation chart is provided for every Chapter Test. Answers for the extended-response questions are on the same page as these charts, and all other answers are provided as annotations on tests.

Test Talk

For every unit, Test Talk helps students learn to use test-taking strategies. Students read a passage about a science topic and then use six strategies to help them answer different types of questions. Each strategy is modeled before students answer questions independently. The *Scott Foresman Science Graphic Organizer and Test Talk Transparency Package* provides transparencies with write-on lines to support the teaching of these strategies.

Writing Prompts

A writing prompt is provided for every unit. In the teacher instruction section, a 6-point scoring rubric is provided along with six anchor papers for each writing prompt.

Performance Test

Each unit includes a science Performance Test. Students go to three stations to complete an investigation and solve a problem. Teacher instructions include a list of materials, preparation suggestions, setup cards for each station, and a scoring guide.

Read each question and choose the best answer.
Then fill in the circle next to the correct answer.

① Choose the word that belongs in the sentence.
_____ have long narrow leaves and do not have woody stems.

Ⓐ Trees

Ⓑ Grasses

Ⓒ Flowers

Ⓓ Evergreens

② What kind of tree grows cones to make seeds?

Ⓕ spring

Ⓖ summer

Ⓗ deciduous

Ⓘ coniferous

③ Choose the word that belongs in the sentence.
Tubes that carry water and minerals from the roots to other parts of the plant are in the _____.

Ⓐ leaf

Ⓑ stem

Ⓒ thorn

Ⓓ flower

④ What structures help keep a cactus from losing too much water?

Ⓕ tubers

Ⓖ thorns

Ⓗ woody stems

Ⓘ stems with a thick, waxy covering

5 Which seed part stores food for the seed?

Ⓐ the fruit

Ⓑ the flower

Ⓒ the seed leaf

Ⓓ the seed coat

6 In the forest, Jan picked burs off her pants and dropped them. What did she do by dropping burs?

Ⓕ She pollinated a plant.

Ⓖ She did nothing important.

Ⓗ She left food for the forest animals.

Ⓘ She helped to scatter a plant's seeds.

7 Look at the illustration below.

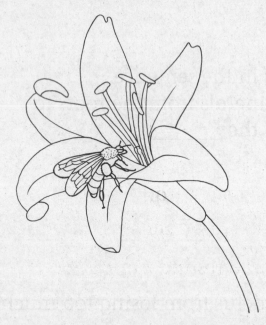

What is the bee doing to the flower?

Ⓐ pollinating it

Ⓑ eating its fruit

Ⓒ germinating it

Ⓓ scattering its seeds

8 Many plants that lived long ago are extinct. How do scientists know about these plants?

    Ⓕ They grow plant fossils.

    Ⓖ They found plant fossils.

    Ⓗ They grow plants like them in space.

    Ⓘ They found living plants that are like them.

9 Look at the object shown in the illustration below.

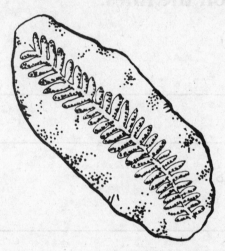

How was this object formed?

    Ⓐ A plant grew in rock.

    Ⓑ A plant was pressed into a rock.

    Ⓒ A plant grew in wood. The wood became rock.

    Ⓓ A plant was pressed into mud. The mud became rock.

10 Scientists have learned many interesting things about plants that lived long ago. What is one difference between early plants and those of today?

    Ⓕ Early plants had more fruit.

    Ⓖ Early plants had more seeds.

    Ⓗ Early plants did not have leaves.

    Ⓘ Early plants did not have flowers.

11 When a seed starts to grow into a new plant, what is it doing?

Ⓐ pollinating

Ⓑ germinating

Ⓒ growing leaves

Ⓓ creating seedlings

Write the answers to the questions on the lines.

12 How do plants get food? (2 points)

_____

_____

13 How do plants get water? (2 points)

_____

_____

Write the answer to the question on a separate sheet of paper.

14 Jacob knows that the different parts of a plant help the plant to live and grow. He decides to put two of the same type of plant in his garden. Both plants get the same amount of water. Jacob covers one plant with a cardboard box. Soon the covered plant appears weak and unhealthy.

Explain why covering the plant with the box prevents it from growing.
(4 points)

**Read each question and choose the best answer.
Then fill in the circle next to the correct answer.**

1 What do sea jellies, earthworms, and spiders have in common?

　Ⓐ They all have eight legs.

　Ⓑ They all have stinging body parts.

　Ⓒ They are all animals with backbones.

　Ⓓ They are all animals without backbones.

2 A pelican's bill has a pouch that hangs from it. How does this adaptation help it survive?

　Ⓕ It helps the bird catch fish.

　Ⓖ It helps the bird store water.

　Ⓗ It helps the bird attack other animals.

　Ⓘ It helps the bird balance itself when it walks.

3 Complete the sentence.
Body parts, such as webbed feet, are inherited, or

　Ⓐ learned.

　Ⓑ never changed.

　Ⓒ passed on from parents to offspring.

　Ⓓ not adapted to different environments.

4 Complete the sentence.
An instinct is a behavior that animals

　Ⓕ copy.

　Ⓖ are born to do.

　Ⓗ teach each other.

　Ⓘ must learn so they can survive.

5 Which sentence is true?

Ⓐ Chimpanzees cannot learn from other chimpanzees.

Ⓑ Chimpanzees have trouble adapting to new environments.

Ⓒ Chimpanzees are born already knowing how to use sticks to capture insects to eat.

Ⓓ Chimpanzees watch other chimpanzees to learn how to use sticks to capture insects to eat.

6 Look at the illustration below. Think about the life cycle of a monarch butterfly.

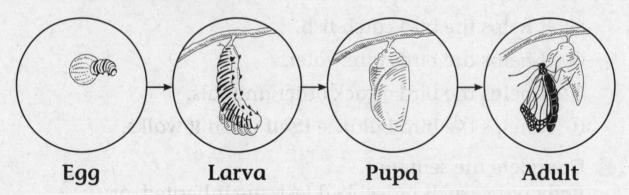

Egg   **Larva**   **Pupa**   **Adult**

What do we usually call a butterfly when it is a larva?

Ⓕ egg

Ⓖ pupa

Ⓗ chrysalis

Ⓘ caterpillar

© Pearson Education, Inc.

7 Which kind of animal usually develops inside its mother?

Ⓐ bird

Ⓑ insect

Ⓒ mammal

Ⓓ amphibian

8 Chris finds something that looks like a rock. It is hard and yellow. A dead insect is inside it. What did Chris most likely find?

Ⓕ a trilobite

Ⓖ a fossil cast

Ⓗ a fossil mold

Ⓘ a piece of amber

9 Look at the illustration below of a *T. rex*. Think about the traits of this dinosaur and the traits of living animals.

What modern-day animal looks like the dinosaur above?

Ⓐ deer

Ⓑ lizard

Ⓒ spider

Ⓓ elephant

10 A walking stick looks like a real twig. What type of adaptation does a walking stick use for protection?

    Ⓕ armor

    Ⓖ poison

    Ⓗ mimicry

    Ⓘ camouflage

Write the answers to the questions on the lines.

11 Amphibians spend part of their lives in water and part on land. Name two members of this group. (2 points)

_____

_____

12 What are the four things all animals need to live? (2 points)

_____

Write the answer to the question on a separate sheet of paper.

13 Long ago, the Badlands of South Dakota were hot and wet. Today the Badlands are dry.

Explain how this change in habitat might harm animals. (4 points)

Read each question and choose the best answer.
Then fill in the circle next to the correct answer.

1 Plants get energy to make food from which of the following?

ⓐ water

ⓑ climate

ⓒ sunlight

ⓓ nutrients

2 Which word best completes the sentence?
Sunlight, water, soil, and climate are the _____ parts of an ecosystem.

ⓕ living

ⓖ growing

ⓗ nonliving

ⓘ interacting

3 Read the paragraph below about a chaparral community. Then answer the question.

Each part of a chaparral community affects the other parts. With a lot of rain, more plants grow in the chaparral. Many animals eat these plants. With much food, the number of animals increases. In dry years, fewer plants grow. With less food, the number of animals decreases.

What happens to the number of animals in years when there is little rain?

ⓐ The number increases.

ⓑ The number decreases.

ⓒ The number does not change.

ⓓ The number decreases and then it increases.

4 Grasshoppers and bison live in which type of ecosystem?

    Ⓕ desert

    Ⓖ tundra

    Ⓗ grasslands

    Ⓘ tropical forest

5 What is the biggest difference between a desert and a tropical forest?

    Ⓐ how cold each gets

    Ⓑ how warm each gets

    Ⓒ how much life each has

    Ⓓ how much rain each gets

6 In which ecosystem would you find wolves, caribou, brown bears, and eagles?

    Ⓕ desert

    Ⓖ prairie

    Ⓗ tundra

    Ⓘ tropical forest

7 Oak, maple, and beech trees drop their leaves in the fall. In which ecosystem are they found?

    Ⓐ tundra

    Ⓑ tropical forest

    Ⓒ deciduous forest

    Ⓓ coniferous forest

© Pearson Education, Inc.

8 Choose the best word to complete the sentence. Lakes, ponds, rivers, and streams are examples of _____ ecosystems.

Ⓕ dry

Ⓖ wetland

Ⓗ saltwater

Ⓘ freshwater

9 Read the chart. Use what you learn to answer the question.

Water Ecosystems	
Type of Water	**Examples of Plants and Animals**
Saltwater	Corals, sea dragons, cuttlefish, clams, crabs, algae, otters, seals, shrimp, whales, starfish
Freshwater	Manatees, bass, cormorants, alligators, red mangrove trees, grasses, bears
Where Freshwater and Saltwater Meet	Fish, crabs

In which type of water would a whale live?

Ⓐ saltwater

Ⓑ freshwater

Ⓒ in any kind of water ecosystem

Ⓓ where freshwater and saltwater meet

Write the answers to the questions on the lines.

❿ Why does a tundra have few trees? (2 points)

_____

_____

⓫ What are two ways plants in an animal's habitat help meet its needs? (2 points)

_____

_____

_____

Write the answer to the question on a separate sheet of paper.

⓬ Look at the illustration below.

Explain ways the coastal redwood trees depend on the nonliving parts of this ecosystem. (4 points)

Name _____

**Read each question and choose the best answer.
Then fill in the circle next to the correct answer.**

1 What is the main reason prairie dogs live together?

Ⓐ for protection

Ⓑ to move faster

Ⓒ for appearance

Ⓓ to raise their young together

2 Which word **best** completes the sentence?
The population of lemmings changes when the amount
of _____ in their environment changes.

Ⓕ habitats

Ⓖ resources

Ⓗ food chains

Ⓘ competition

3 Which word **best** completes the sentence?
A _____ is a living thing that breaks down waste
and things that have died.

Ⓐ predator

Ⓑ producer

Ⓒ consumer

Ⓓ decomposer

4 Small trees trying to get the same resources as taller trees is
an example of which of the following?

Ⓕ producers

Ⓖ consumers

Ⓗ interaction

Ⓘ competition

5 Look at the chart below. Think about how each living thing gets the energy it needs to live.

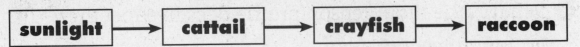

Which term describes the food-getting interactions among the living things in this chart?

Ⓐ food web

Ⓑ producers

Ⓒ food chain

Ⓓ consumers

6 In which part of the digestive system does most digestion happen?

Ⓕ mouth

Ⓖ stomach

Ⓗ large intestine

Ⓘ small intestine

7 When plants burn, they can turn to ash. How does the ash left by a fire affect other plants?

Ⓐ It has no effect.

Ⓑ It helps plants grow.

Ⓒ It stops plants from growing.

Ⓓ It prevents new plants from growing.

8 Look at the illustration below. It shows a place that was once dry.

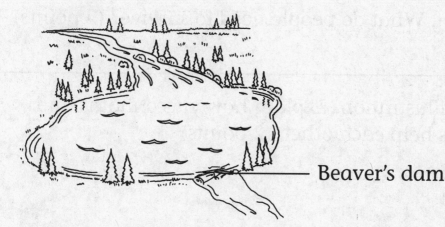

Beaver's dam

How did a beaver's dam change the environment?

Ⓕ There is more grass.

Ⓖ There are more fish.

Ⓗ There are fewer trees.

Ⓘ There are more flowers.

9 Choose the term that belongs in the sentence.

_____ keeps a person's heart, lungs, and muscles strong.

Ⓐ Sitting

Ⓑ Exercise

Ⓒ Clean air

Ⓓ Sugary food

10 What is one way to stop the spread of germs?

Ⓕ Never go outside.

Ⓖ Always wear a jacket.

Ⓗ Wash your hands often.

Ⓘ Never go outside when it is cold.

Write the answers to the questions on the lines.

11 People obtain the things they need to live from the environment. What do people need to survive? (2 points)

_____

12 Look at the illustration. Explain how yucca moths and yucca plants help each other. (2 points)

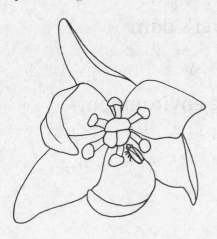

_____

_____

_____

Write the answer to the question on a separate sheet of paper.

13 In a food web, prairie dogs eat grass. Ferrets eat the prairie dogs. Golden eagles eat prairie dogs and mice. Badgers eat the ferrets. Ranchers brought cattle into the food web and removed many prairie dogs. How did the ranchers' actions affect the other animals?
(4 points)

**Read each question and choose the best answer.
Then fill in the circle next to the correct answer.**

1 Plants need leaves to

Ⓐ shade the plant from the Sun.

Ⓑ make sugar as food for the plant.

Ⓒ take in water for the plant to live.

Ⓓ make carbon dioxide for us to breathe.

2 What plant part takes water and minerals from the soil, holds the plant in its place, and stores food?

Ⓕ seeds

Ⓖ leaves

Ⓗ root system

Ⓘ stem system

3 Look at the illustration below.

What kind of tree does the picture show?

Ⓐ grassy

Ⓑ coniferous

Ⓒ evergreen

Ⓓ deciduous

4 A pika is a vertebrate animal that has hair, breathes air through its lungs, and feeds milk to its young. What animal group does a pika belong to?

   Ⓕ fish

   Ⓖ birds

   Ⓗ reptiles

   Ⓘ mammals

5 A bear does not have to learn how to hibernate. Knowing how to hibernate is

   Ⓐ an instinct.

   Ⓑ an adaptation.

   Ⓒ a practiced skill.

   Ⓓ a previously learned trait.

6 How does a mammal usually develop?

   Ⓕ as a larva

   Ⓖ as a tadpole

   Ⓗ inside its mother

   Ⓘ inside a chrysalis

7 If a habitat does not have the right kind of food for a certain kind of animal, what is most likely to happen?

   Ⓐ The animal will change its diet.

   Ⓑ The animal will bring its own food.

   Ⓒ The animal will move to a new habitat.

   Ⓓ The animal will have its young there but not live there.

8 Grasshoppers eat grass. Which ecosystem is best for grasshoppers?

Ⓗ forest

Ⓘ desert

Ⓙ tundra

Ⓚ grassland

9 A bass lives among the weeds of lakes and streams. Which water ecosystem is best for a bass?

Ⓐ pond

Ⓑ saltwater

Ⓒ freshwater

Ⓓ where freshwater and saltwater mix

10 Look at the illustration below.

How do prairie dogs interact with their group?

Ⓗ They hunt for food together.

Ⓘ They run away from the group.

Ⓙ They prefer to live away from the group.

Ⓚ They stand watch and warn the group of danger.

⑪ Living things that eat plants and animals are called

    Ⓐ producers.

    Ⓑ carnivores.

    Ⓒ omnivores.

    Ⓓ herbivores.

Write the answers to the questions on the lines.

⑫ List the following plants and animals in the order that they would be in a food chain: ferret, prairie dog, bobcat, grass (2 points)

_____

_____

⑬ A tree in a forest fell to the ground and started decaying. Why is it a good idea to leave the tree there and not remove it? (2 points)

_____

_____

Write your answers to the question on a separate sheet of paper.

⑭ Several of your classmates have the flu. Some stay home. Some come to school.

Explain which is the better thing to do and why. Also name something you can do to stop the spread of germs. (4 points)

Paul Sereno: Expert Dinosaur Hunter

Directions: Read about an expert dinosaur hunter. Then follow the directions on pages 22–27.

As a boy, Paul Sereno liked to go on nature hikes with his brothers. He brought home insects to add to his collection. Paul went to college to study art. However, while he was in college, Paul decided he wanted to become a paleontologist—a scientist who studies ancient life.

Paleontologists like Dr. Sereno try to find fossils to piece together the story of what life was like long ago. Dr. Sereno and his team have found many new kinds of dinosaurs.

They found one of their greatest discoveries in Africa. A giant claw lying on the desert floor was the first clue. Dr. Sereno and his team carefully dug for more bones. They revealed a huge skeleton of a new kind of dinosaur. Its skull was long with crocodile-like teeth. Dr. Sereno named the new dinosaur *Suchomimus*, which means "crocodile mimic."

It sometimes takes years for paleontologists to make sense of what they find. But their hard work usually pays off. Every year new discoveries continue to fill out our picture of the past.

Strategy 1 Locate Key Words in the Question

Directions: Before you can answer a question, you need to understand it. Follow these steps to understand the question.

- Read the question.
- Ask yourself: "**Who** or **what** is the question about?" Words that tell "who" or "what" are **key words**. Circle key words.
- Look for and circle other key words. Often question words and other important words are key words.
- Turn the question into a statement using key words. Follow this model: "I need to find out _____."

Learn

Read the question. Circle the key words and then complete the sentence.

1. (While) he was (in college,) (what) did (Paul Sereno decide) to (become)?

   Ⓐ an artist   Ⓒ a paleontologist

   Ⓑ a dentist   Ⓓ a crocodile hunter

   I need to find out <u>what Paul Sereno decided to</u>

   <u>become while he was in college.</u>

   > • Turn the question into a statement using key words.

Try It

Read each question. Circle the key words and answer each question.

2. What did Paul Sereno do with his brothers when he was young?

   Ⓐ went on nature hikes

   Ⓑ collected dinosaur bones

   Ⓒ searched for life in the desert

   Ⓓ named new kinds of reptiles they found

   I need to find out _____

   _____

3. What is a paleontologist? Use details from the text to support your answer.

   I need to find out _____

   _____

Name _____

Strategy 2 Locate Key Words in the Text

Directions: You can also understand a question by thinking about where you need to look for the answer. Follow these steps to understand the question.

- Read the question.
- Look for and **circle key words** in the question.
- Look for and circle key words in the text that match key words in the question.
- Decide where to look for the answer.
  - To find the answer, you may have to **look in one place in the text**. The answer is *right there* in the text.
  - To find the answer, you may have to **look in several places in the text**. You have to *think* and *search* for information.
  - To find the answer, you may have to **combine what you know with what the author tells you**. The answer comes from the *author* and *you*.

Learn

Read the question. Circle the key words and then complete the sentence.

1. (While) he was (in college) (what) did (Paul Sereno) (decide) to (become)?

   I found the answer in paragraph 1, sentence 4.

- Look for and circle key words in the question.
- Look for and circle key words in the text that match key words in the question.

Try It

Read each question. Circle the key words and answer the question.

- The question asks what Paul Sereno decided to become when he was in college.
- You will have to look in one place in the text for information.

2. What did Paul Sereno do with his brothers when he was young?
   Ⓐ went on nature hikes
   Ⓑ collected dinosaur bones
   Ⓒ searched for life in the desert
   Ⓓ named new kinds of reptiles they found

   I found the answer in _____

3. What do paleontologists do? Use details from the text to support your answer.

   I found the answer in _____

   _____

© Pearson Education, Inc.

Strategy 3 Choose the Right Answer

Directions: Use this strategy for a multiple-choice question in which you are not positive of the right answer.

- Read the question.
- Read each answer choice.
- **Rule out** any choice you know is wrong. Go back to the text to rule out other choices.
- Mark your answer choice.
- **Check your answer** by comparing it with the text.

Learn

Cross out any choice you know is wrong. Next, go back to the text to rule out any other choices. Then mark your choice.

1. While he was in college what did Paul Sereno decide to become?
   Ⓐ ~~an artist~~
   Ⓑ ~~a dentist~~
   Ⓒ a paleontologist
   Ⓓ ~~a crocodile hunter~~

- Look for this subject in the text.

- Rule out incorrect choices. Choose answer C because the text supports this choice.

Try It

Cross out any choice you know is wrong. Next, go back to the text to rule out any other choices. Then mark your answer.

2. What did Paul Sereno do with his brothers when he was young?
   Ⓕ went on nature hikes
   Ⓖ collected dinosaur bones
   Ⓗ searched for life in the desert
   Ⓘ named new kinds of reptiles they found

3. What is a paleontologist?
   Ⓐ someone who studies art
   Ⓑ someone who studies crocodiles
   Ⓒ a scientist who collects insects
   Ⓓ a scientist who studies ancient life

Name _____

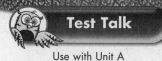

Strategy 4 Use Information from the Text

Directions: A question may ask you to support your answer with details from the text. If it does, then you must include information from the text. Follow these steps to understand questions like this.

- Read the question.
- Look for and circle key words in the question.
- **Make notes** about details from the text that answer the question.
- Reread the question and your notes.
- If details are missing, go back to the text.

Learn

Use information from the text to answer the question.

1. While he was in college what did Paul Sereno decide to become? Use details from the text to support your answer.

   My Notes: a paleontologist, a scientist who studies ancient life.

   My Answer: While in college, Paul Sereno decided to become a paleontologist. He wanted to be a scientist who studies ancient life.

- Circle key words in the question. The question asks you to tell what Paul Sereno decided to become when he was in college.

- Read text and make notes about paleontologists and the work they do.

Try It

2. What do paleontologists do? Use details from the text to support your answer.

   My Notes: _____

   _____

   _____

   My Answer: _____

   _____

   _____

   _____

Strategy 5 Use Information from Graphics

Directions: A question may ask you about a picture or ask you to support your answer with details from a picture or pictures. If it does, you must include information from the picture. Follow these instructions to answer questions about a picture.

- Read the question.
- Look for and circle key words in the question.
- Use what you know to analyze the picture.
- Use details from the picture to answer the question.

Learn

Look at the picture on page 21. Use information from the picture to answer the question.

1. Based on the picture, what did Suchomimus look like? Use details to support your answer.

   • Look for and circle key words in the question.

   To find the answer, I will look at the picture to see what Suchomimus looked like.

   My Answer: Suchomimus looked like a big dinosaur with a long skull and the teeth of a crocodile.

Try It

Look at the picture on page 21. Use information from the picture to answer the question.

2. Based on the picture, tell where fossils can sometimes be found. Use details to support your answer.

   To find the answer, I will _____

   _____

   _____

   My Answer: _____

   _____

   _____

Strategy 6 Write Your Answer to Score High

Directions: A question may ask you to write an answer. Make sure to write a correct, complete, and focused answer.

Learn

Look at this sample written by an imaginary student named Carla. Analyze Carla's work. Cross out incorrect information. What should she do to score higher?

1. ⟨What⟩ did ⟨Dr. Sereno's team find⟩ in ⟨Africa⟩? Use details from the text and picture.

   Carla's Notes: a giant claw on the desert floor ~~a crocodile~~, Suchomimus, long skull, crocodile-like teeth.

   Carla's Answer: Dr. Sereno and his team found a giant claw on the desert floor in Africa. It was from a crocodile named Suchomimus. It has a long skull and crocodile teeth. When he was young, Paul Sereno collected insects.

   To score higher, Carla needs to change "crocodile" to "dinosaur" because "crocodile" is wrong. She also needs to take out "When he was young, Paul Sereno collected insects" because that is not important.

- Carla circled words in the question.
- Carla's notes have errors.
- Carla's answer has information that is wrong and is not important.

Try It

Look at this sample done by an imaginary student named Derek. Analyze Derek's work. Cross out incorrect information. What should he do to score higher?

2. How does the hard work done by paleontologists usually pay off? Explain your answer using details from the text.

   Derek's Notes: may take years to make sense, why do they do it? new discoveries every year, fill in picture of the past.

   Derek's Answer: Paleontologists have to study hard when they are in college. Paleontologists may work hard for years before they can make sense of what they find. A giant tooth is a clue. But every year new discoveries help them.

   To score higher, Derek needs to _____

   _____

   _____

© Pearson Education, Inc.

Grade 3 Writing Prompt

Read the writing prompt in the box. Write on a separate sheet of paper.

Choose an ecosystem. Write a story that tells about the plants and animals that live there. Include details about how the plants and animals interact.

The information in the box below will help you remember what you should think about when you write your composition.

REMEMBER—YOU SHOULD
- ❑ write the main ideas that answer the question about the ecosystem, including the details that support each idea.
- ❑ present your ideas logically and in an organized way.
- ❑ choose words that say exactly what you want to say.
- ❑ write complete sentences, and make sure that your sentences are varied.
- ❑ check for correct spelling, grammar, punctuation, and word usage.

Collecting Data on Bottled Water

Decide if two different water sources should be used for bottled water.

Station 1

Use the card at the station to correctly set up the equipment.

Water Sample Observation

Pour water from bottle A into cup A up to the fill line. Do the same with bottle B and cup B.

Observe how the water in each sample looks and smells.

Record your observations of water samples A and B.

Sample A: _____

Sample B: _____

Station 2

Use the card at the station to correctly set up the equipment.

Water Test 1

Pour sample A through funnel A into cup A. Do the same with sample B, funnel B, and cup B.

Observe each filter and each sample of filtered water.

Record your observations of water samples A and B.

Sample A: _____

Sample B: _____

Station 3

Use the card at the station to correctly set up the equipment.

Water Test 2

Use the litmus paper to test each sample. Compare the color of your litmus strips with the color of the litmus strip labeled "standard."

Record your observations in the data table.

Water sample	Clearness	Odor	Reacts with litmus paper
Standard			
Sample A			
Sample B			

Data Analysis

Now you have completed the water tests. Use your data and what you know about water to answer the following question.

Would either of the two sources provide water that would be good drinking water? Explain.

_____

_____

_____

_____

Read each question and choose the best answer.
Then fill in the circle next to the correct answer.

1 What makes up two-thirds of your body?

Ⓐ skin

Ⓑ water

Ⓒ oxygen

Ⓓ muscles

2 Choose the term that belongs in the sentence.
People use the power of moving water to make _____.

Ⓕ electricity

Ⓖ generators

Ⓗ wind power

Ⓘ solar power

3 About how much of Earth's surface is covered with water?

Ⓐ 10%

Ⓑ 25%

Ⓒ 67%

Ⓓ 75%

4 What is water that seeps down and collects in underground spaces called?

Ⓕ saltwater

Ⓖ well water

Ⓗ water vapor

Ⓘ groundwater

5 Why are wetlands an important environmental resource?

Ⓐ They help to flood dry areas.

Ⓑ They are homes for many animals.

Ⓒ They decrease the water vapor supply.

Ⓓ They decrease the groundwater supply.

6 What process occurs when water changes to a gas?

Ⓕ melting

Ⓖ evaporation

Ⓗ precipitation

Ⓘ condensation

7 At what temperature does water freeze solid?

Ⓐ 0°C

Ⓑ 10°C

Ⓒ 32°C

Ⓓ 100°C

8 During the water cycle, what generally happens to the water after evaporation?

Ⓕ It falls to Earth as precipitation.

Ⓖ It condenses and forms a cloud.

Ⓗ It evaporates until it is entirely gone.

Ⓘ It seeps into Earth as groundwater.

9 Look at the illustration below.

What will happen to the water in the plastic bottle when it freezes?

Ⓐ It will expand.

Ⓑ It will contract.

Ⓒ It will evaporate.

Ⓓ It will remain the same.

10 What kind of water is found in the air?

Ⓕ saltwater

Ⓖ well water

Ⓗ water vapor

Ⓘ groundwater

11 Choose the words that complete the sentence.
Some of the chemicals that are added to water at a water-treatment area _____.

Ⓐ kill germs

Ⓑ remove dirt

Ⓒ harm your teeth

Ⓓ turn water into water vapor

Write the answer to the question on the lines.

12 Why must water that people use be clean? Give two reasons. (2 points)

_____

_____

Write the answer to the question on a separate sheet of paper.

13 Look at the illustration below.

Part A Label the three arrows on the picture identifying precipitation, evaporation, and condensation.

Part B Describe what occurs during precipitation, evaporation, and condensation. (4 points)

**Read each question and choose the best answer.
Then fill in the circle next to the correct answer.**

1 On what kind of day would you see white, fluffy clouds?

Ⓐ a cold, snowy day

Ⓑ a cool, stormy day

Ⓒ a warm, rainy day

Ⓓ a warm, bright day

2 What type of winter weather will there likely be in a town in eastern Washington?

Ⓕ The weather will be cold and dry.

Ⓖ The weather will be cool and wet.

Ⓗ The weather will be mild and wet.

Ⓘ The weather will be warm and dry.

3 Look at the illustration below.

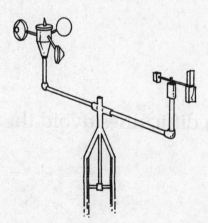

What do scientists measure using the tool shown?

Ⓐ rainfall

Ⓑ humidity

Ⓒ wind speed

Ⓓ air pressure

❹ A scientist needs to measure the air pressure. What tool should the scientist use?

Ⓕ barometer

Ⓖ rain gauge

Ⓗ hygrometer

Ⓘ thermometer

❺ What type of severe storm is a spinning column of air that touches the ground?

Ⓐ tornado

Ⓑ blizzard

Ⓒ hurricane

Ⓓ thunderstorm

❻ Where do hurricanes form?

Ⓕ over deserts

Ⓖ over dry land

Ⓗ over ice sheets

Ⓘ over warm oceans

❼ When should people with breathing difficulties avoid the outdoors?

Ⓐ when there is acid rain

Ⓑ when there is a smog alert

Ⓒ when there is heavy snowfall

Ⓓ when there is a thunderstorm watch

© Pearson Education, Inc.

8 What harmful substance do cars and trucks cause in the air?

ⓕ ozone

ⓖ oxygen

ⓗ nitrogen

ⓘ carbon dioxide

9 If the National Weather Service puts out a tornado warning, when is a tornado likely to strike?

Ⓐ in a few days

Ⓑ in a few hours

Ⓒ during the next month

Ⓓ during the next few minutes

10 What does a picture of the sun behind a cloud mean on a weather map?

ⓕ rainy weather

ⓖ sunny weather

ⓗ stormy weather

ⓘ partly cloudy weather

11 What type of storm has low temperatures, strong winds, and heavy snowfall?

Ⓐ cyclone

Ⓑ tornado

Ⓒ blizzard

Ⓓ hurricane

Write the answers to the question on the lines.

12 A scientist is using the instrument shown below. What is the name of the instrument? What is it used for? (2 points)

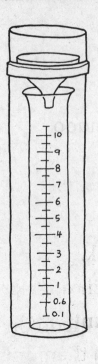

_____

_____

_____

Write the answer to the question on a separate sheet of paper.

13 Some storms can be very dangerous.

Part A Describe the features of a hurricane.

Part B Compare a hurricane to a tornado. Explain how they are alike and different. (4 points)

**Read each question and choose the best answer.
Then fill in the circle next to the correct answer.**

1 One way to tell rocks apart is by looking at the size of the bits of minerals that make up each rock. What is this physical property called?

Ⓐ color

Ⓑ luster

Ⓒ texture

Ⓓ heaviness

2 How is metamorphic rock formed?

Ⓕ Pressure over time binds sediments into rock.

Ⓖ Heat and/or pressure change the minerals in a rock.

Ⓗ A hot mixture of gases and minerals cools into rock.

Ⓘ Water slowly wears down minerals, turning them into rock.

3 Look at the illustration below.

What type of rock is shown?

Ⓐ shale

Ⓑ igneous

Ⓒ sedimentary

Ⓓ metamorphic

4 Which type of particles found in soil are the smallest?

Ⓕ silt

Ⓖ clay

Ⓗ sand

Ⓘ shale

5 What layer of soil includes rock particles mixed with the dark products of decay?

Ⓐ silt

Ⓑ clay

Ⓒ topsoil

Ⓓ subsoil

6 What mineral is crushed and ground into salt that is used to season food?

Ⓕ halite

Ⓖ quartz

Ⓗ fluorite

Ⓘ graphite

7 Which two properties would be best to use to identify a mineral?

Ⓐ color and luster

Ⓑ shape and luster

Ⓒ size and magnetism

Ⓓ hardness and streak

8 Where do the nutrients in the soil mainly come from?

Ⓡ rainfall

Ⓢ running water

Ⓣ living plants and animals

Ⓤ decay of plants and animals

9 Look at the illustration below.

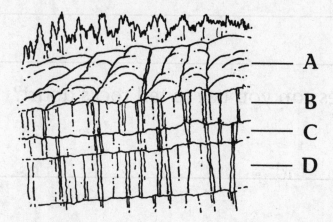

In which layer will the oldest fossils most likely be found?

Ⓐ A

Ⓑ B

Ⓒ C

Ⓓ D

10 What is rock called that is formed from bits of rocky matter that settle to the bottom of rivers, lakes, and oceans?

Ⓡ shale

Ⓢ igneous

Ⓣ sedimentary

Ⓤ metamorphic

Write the answers to the questions on the lines.

11 Why is the mixture of soil called loam good for growing plants? (2 points)

_____

_____

_____

_____

12 What physical properties can you use to tell rocks apart? (2 points)

_____

_____

_____

Write the answer to the question on a separate sheet of paper.

13 People use minerals almost every day. Identify four ways that you have used minerals today. (4 points)

**Read each question and choose the best answer.
Then fill in the circle next to the correct answer.**

1 Look at the illustration below.

What layer of Earth is the arrow pointing to?

Ⓐ core

Ⓑ crust

Ⓒ mantle

Ⓓ inner core

2 What forms when water slows enough to fill an area?

Ⓕ lake

Ⓖ river

Ⓗ waterfall

Ⓘ stream

3 What landform is made when a river slowly cuts through rock?

Ⓐ hill

Ⓑ plain

Ⓒ valley

Ⓓ mountain

4 What force can rapidly change the Earth's landscape?

Ⓕ wind erosion

Ⓖ weathering

Ⓗ thunderstorms

Ⓘ volcanic eruptions

5 When igneous rock from a volcanic eruption cools, what does it form?

Ⓐ new core

Ⓑ new crust

Ⓒ new mantle

Ⓓ new inner core

6 How does water break apart a rock?

Ⓕ It takes up less space when it freezes in cold weather.

Ⓖ It takes up less space when it melts in warm weather.

Ⓗ It takes up more space when it freezes in cold weather.

Ⓘ It takes up more space when it melts in warm weather.

7 What carries soil away from hilly farm fields?

Ⓐ rain

Ⓑ plants

Ⓒ rivers

Ⓓ waves

© Pearson Education, Inc.

8 What causes a rockslide—the quick movement of rocks down a slope?

Ⓕ wind

Ⓖ water

Ⓗ gravity

Ⓘ glaciers

9 How does erosion **mainly** occur in dry regions?

Ⓐ Gravity pulls soil downhill.

Ⓑ Mud flows quickly down a slope.

Ⓒ Sand particles blow against rocks.

Ⓓ Rock particles are carried away by water.

10 Look at the illustration below.

The picture shows rock breaking into smaller and smaller pieces. What force causes this change?

Ⓕ erosion

Ⓖ gravity

Ⓗ flooding

Ⓘ weathering

Write the answers to the questions on the lines.

11 Explain how an earthquake can change Earth's surface. (2 points)

_____

_____

_____

_____

12 As a tree grows, it can cause weathering. Explain how the roots of a tree cause weathering. (2 points)

_____

_____

_____

_____

Write the answer to the question on a separate sheet of paper.

13 Earth's surface is constantly changing. Describe how erosion and weathering change Earth's surface. Explain how the processes are alike and different. (4 points)

Name _____

**Read each question and choose the best answer.
Then fill in the circle next to the correct answer.**

1 Important materials from Earth that living things need
are called

Ⓐ natural resources.

Ⓑ necessary resources.

Ⓒ renewable resources.

Ⓓ nonrenewable resources.

2 Which of the following is a nonrenewable resource?

Ⓕ coal

Ⓖ trees

Ⓗ wind

Ⓘ water

3 Choose the term that belongs in the sentence.

_____ is a resource that cannot be used up.

Ⓐ Oil

Ⓑ Coal

Ⓒ A tree

Ⓓ Sunlight

4 Which of the following is an example of recycling
a resource?

Ⓕ drinking water instead of milk

Ⓖ adding chocolate sauce to white milk

Ⓗ making a flower pot out of a milk jug

Ⓘ buying milk in quarts instead of gallons

5 Look at the illustration below.

The picture shows a water pipe pouring water into a wetland. How will the wetland help conserve water?

Ⓐ The wetland cleans dirty water.

Ⓑ The wetland absorbs all the water.

Ⓒ The wetland holds back dirty water.

Ⓓ The wetland releases water into the oceans.

6 Which of the following is a nonrenewable resource that contains metals or other minerals that people use?

Ⓕ oil

Ⓖ ore

Ⓗ gas

Ⓘ coal

7 Which of the following makes up **most** of our trash?

Ⓐ glass

Ⓑ paper

Ⓒ plastic

Ⓓ metal cans

8 Using natural resources wisely so we do not waste them is called

Ⓕ reusing.

Ⓖ recycling.

Ⓗ containment.

Ⓘ conservation.

9 Look at the illustration below.

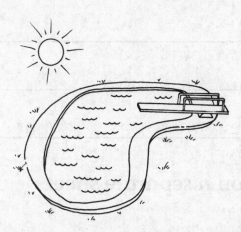

What type of resource is warming the swimming pool?

Ⓐ natural, renewable resource

Ⓑ natural, nonrenewable resource

Ⓒ human-made, renewable resource

Ⓓ human-made, nonrenewable resource

Write the answers to the questions on the lines.

10 Describe two ways that the amount of landfill space can be reduced. (2 points)

_____

_____

_____

11 Identify four things that you can reuse instead of throwing away. Explain how you will reuse each item. (2 points)

_____

_____

_____

_____

Write the answer to the question on a separate sheet of paper.

12 Trees are an important natural resource.

Part A Tell if trees are a renewable or nonrenewable resource. Explain your answer.

Part B Name two ways people use trees as a resource. (4 points)

**Read each question and choose the best answer.
Then fill in the circle next to the correct answer.**

1 A liquid changes into a gas during which process?

Ⓐ melting

Ⓑ evaporation

Ⓒ precipitation

Ⓓ condensation

2 What type of rock has been changed by heat and/or pressure?

Ⓕ humus rock

Ⓖ igneous rock

Ⓗ sedimentary rock

Ⓘ metamorphic rock

3 What is the main cause of change to most landforms?

Ⓐ gravity

Ⓑ weathering

Ⓒ erosion by wind

Ⓓ erosion by water

4 Which of the following is the hardest mineral on Earth?

Ⓕ mica

Ⓖ crocoite

Ⓗ diamond

Ⓘ molybdenite

5 Look at the illustration below.

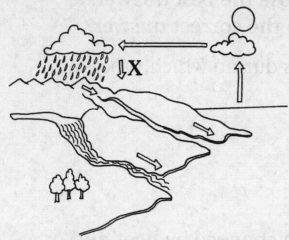

The arrow with an "X" shows which process?

Ⓐ evaporation

Ⓑ precipitation

Ⓒ stream water flow

Ⓓ groundwater flow

6 Choose the words that belong in the sentence.

The innermost layer of Earth is the _____, which is made of _____.

Ⓕ core, gas

Ⓖ core, metal

Ⓗ crust, rocks

Ⓘ mantle, minerals

7 A town in the southern United States receives most of its weather from the Gulf of Mexico. What type of summer weather is the town most likely to have?

Ⓐ cool and dry

Ⓑ cool and wet

Ⓒ warm and dry

Ⓓ warm and wet

8 Look at the illustration below.

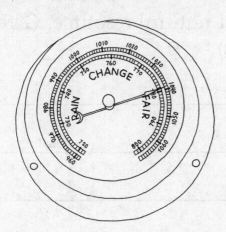

What does this weather tool measure?

(F) rainfall

(G) air pressure

(H) temperature

(I) wind direction

9 In what layer of soil would you find the greatest amount of decayed material?

(A) silt

(B) clay

(C) topsoil

(D) subsoil

10 Which of the following is a renewable resource?

(F) oil

(G) coal

(H) water

(I) iron ore

© Pearson Education, Inc.

Write the answers to the questions on the lines.

11 Explain why trees are an important natural resource. Give examples in your answer. (2 points)

_____

_____

_____

_____

12 Volcanoes rapidly change Earth's surface. Describe how a volcano affects Earth's surface. (2 points)

_____

_____

_____

_____

Write your answers to the question on a separate sheet of paper.

13 Reusing, reducing, and recycling natural resources are important ways to conserve land and to care for the Earth.

Explain what people do when they reuse, reduce, and recycle natural resources. Then give an example of how you can use each method. (4 points)

© Pearson Education, Inc.

Name _____

Studying Clouds From Space

Directions: Read about how NASA studies clouds from space. Then follow the directions on pages 56–61.

You know that NASA studies space. NASA also studies Earth's clouds from space. NASA satellites orbit Earth and use different tools to collect information about clouds and other parts of weather. Some of the tools measure the amount of sunlight that bounces off clouds. Other tools measure how much heat is trapped in clouds and how much goes into space.

cumulus clouds

Clouds are an important part of weather patterns. They are part of the water cycle. They interact with the gases that trap heat and warm Earth. NASA scientists are studying how clouds affect Earth's weather over a long period of time.

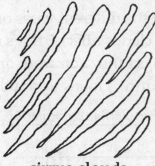

cirrus clouds

Many schools are helping NASA study clouds. Students and teachers at these schools observe and measure parts of the weather. They are given times to record the kinds of clouds and the temperature. These times are when tools on a NASA satellite are recording information for their area. NASA then studies the information.

stratocumulus clouds

Strategy 1 Locate Key Words in the Question

Directions: Before you can answer a question, you need to understand it. Follow these steps to understand the question.

- Read the question.
- Ask yourself: "**Who** or **what** is the question about?" Words that tell "who" or "what" are **key words**. Circle key words.
- Look for and circle other key words. Often question words and other important words are key words.
- Turn the question into a statement using key words. Follow this model: "I need to find out _____."

Learn

Read the question. Circle the key words and then complete the sentence.

1. (Why) do (NASA scientists) want to (collect information) about (Earth's clouds) from (space)?
   - Ⓐ They want to identify all the different types of clouds.
   - Ⓑ They want to know how clouds affect Earth's weather.
   - Ⓒ They want to have a project they can work on with students.
   - Ⓓ They want to compare Earth's clouds to clouds on other planets.

   I need to find out <u>why NASA scientists collect</u>
   <u>information from space about Earth's clouds.</u>

   - Turn the question into a statement using key words.

Try It

Read each question. Circle the key words and answer each question.

2. When do students record information for NASA?
   - Ⓐ at assigned times
   - Ⓑ before school each day
   - Ⓒ when they see the satellite
   - Ⓓ every two hours during the day

   I need to find out _____

   _____

3. How are clouds part of the water cycle? Use details from the text to support your answer.

   I need to find out _____

Strategy 2 Locate Key Words in the Text

Directions: You can also understand a question by thinking about where you need to look for the answer. Follow these steps to understand the question.

- Read the question.
- Look for and **circle key words** in the question.
- Look for and circle key words in the text that match key words in the question.
- Decide where to look for the answer.
  - To find the answer, you may have to **look in one place in the text**. The answer is *right there* in the text.
  - To find the answer, you may have to **look in several places in the text**. You have to *think* and *search* for information.
  - To find the answer, you may have to **combine what you know with what the author tells you**. The answer comes from the *author* and *you*.

Learn

Read the question. Circle the key words and then complete the sentence.

1. (Why) do (NASA scientists) want to (collect) (information) about (Earth's clouds) from (space)?

   I found the answer in <u>paragraph 2, sentence 4.</u>

- Look for and circle key words in the question.
- Look for and circle key words in the text that match key words in the question.

- The question asks why NASA scientists want to study Earth's clouds from space.
- You will have to look in one place in the text for information.

Try It

Read each question. Circle the key words and answer the question.

2. When do students record information for NASA?
   - Ⓐ at assigned times
   - Ⓑ before school each day
   - Ⓒ when they see the satellite
   - Ⓓ every two hours during the day

   I found the answer in _____

3. How are clouds part of the water cycle? Use details from the text to support your answer.

   I found the answer in _____

Strategy 3 Choose the Right Answer

Directions: Use this strategy for a multiple-choice question in which you are not positive of the right answer.

- Read the question.
- Read each answer choice.
- **Rule out** any choice you know is wrong. Go back to the text to rule out other choices.
- Mark your answer choice.
- **Check your answer** by comparing it with the text.

Learn

Cross out any choice you know is wrong. Next, go back to the text to rule out any other choices. Then mark your choice.

1. Why do NASA scientists want to collect information about Earth's clouds from space?

   Ⓐ ~~They want to identify all the different types of clouds.~~

   Ⓑ They want to know how clouds affect Earth's weather.

   Ⓒ ~~They want to have a project they can work on with students.~~

   Ⓓ ~~They want to compare Earth's clouds to clouds on other planets.~~

- Look for this subject in the text.

- Rule out incorrect choices. Choose answer B because the text supports this choice.

Try It

Cross out any choice you know is wrong. Next, go back to the text to rule out any other choices. Then mark your answer.

2. When do students record information for NASA?

   Ⓕ at assigned times

   Ⓖ before school each day

   Ⓗ when they see the satellite

   Ⓘ every two hours during the day

3. How are clouds part of the water cycle?

   Ⓐ They reflect the warmth of Earth into space.

   Ⓑ They work with gases that trap heat and warm Earth.

   Ⓒ They block the warmth of the Sun from reaching Earth.

   Ⓓ They trap heat to prevent the heat from reaching Earth.

Name _____

Strategy 4 Use Information from the Text

Directions: A question may ask you to support your answer with details from the text. If it does, then you must include information from the text. Follow these steps to understand questions like this.

- Read the question.
- Look for and circle key words in the question.
- **Make notes** about details from the text that answer the question.
- Reread the question and your notes.
- If details are missing, go back to the text.

Learn

Use information from the text to answer the question.

1. (Why) do (NASA scientists) want to (collect) (information) about (Earth's clouds) from (space)? Use details from the text to support your answer.

   My Notes: use tools from satellites to collect information about clouds and weather, clouds are part of water cycle, studying how clouds affect Earth's weather

   - Circle key words in the question. The question asks you to explain why NASA scientists collect information about Earth's clouds from space.

   - Read text and make notes about the information NASA scientists collect about clouds.

   My Answer: NASA scientists collect information about Earth's clouds using tools on satellites. They use this information to help them study how clouds affect Earth's weather.

Try It

2. How are clouds part of the water cycle? Use details from the text to support your answer.

   My Notes: _____

   _____

   My Answer: _____

   _____

   _____

Name _____

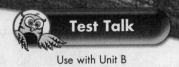
Strategy 5 Use Information from Graphics

Directions: A question may ask you about a picture or ask you to support your answer with details from a picture or pictures. If it does, you must include information from the picture. Follow these instructions to answer questions about a picture.

- Read the question.
- Look for and circle key words in the question.
- Use what you know to analyze the picture.
- Use details from the picture to answer the question.

Learn

Look at the pictures on page 55. Use information from these pictures to answer the question.

1. Based on the (pictures), how are (cumulus) and (cirrus clouds different)? Use details to support your answer.

   > - Look for and circle key words in the question.

   To find the answer, I will <u>find the pictures of cumulus and cirrus clouds and</u>
   <u>then compare what each type of cloud looks like.</u>

   My Answer: <u>Cumulus clouds are puffy and thick while cirrus clouds are</u>
   <u>thinner and wispy.</u>

Try It

Look at the pictures on page 55. Use information from the pictures to answer the question.

2. Based on the pictures, why do some clouds have names that are combinations of two other types of clouds, such as stratocumulus? Use details to support your answer.

   To find the answer, I will _____

   _____

   _____

   My Answer: _____

   _____

   _____

60 Unit B Test Talk

Assessment Book

Name _____

Strategy 6 Write Your Answer to Score High

Directions: A question may ask you to write an answer. Make sure to write a correct, complete, and focused answer.

Learn

Look at this sample written by an imaginary student named Dylan. Analyze Dylan's work. Cross out incorrect information. What should he do to score higher?

1. What information do the tools used to study clouds collect? Use details from the text to support your answer.

- Dylan circled words in the question.

Dylan's Notes: collect information about clouds, weather, ~~clouds are part of weather cycle,~~ amount of sunlight that bounces off clouds, amount of heat in clouds, amount of heat that goes into space, ~~type of weather occurring in the world.~~

- Dylan's notes have information that is not important and is wrong.

Dylan's Answer: The tools NASA uses to study clouds collect information about the clouds, weather, weather cycle, and the type of weather occurring in the world. These tools measure the amount of sunlight that bounces off clouds and the amount of heat trapped in clouds.

- Dylan's answer has inaccurate information and is unfocused.

To score higher, Dylan needs to <u>take out the information about the weather cycle and weather occurring in the world. Dylan could also add a line about how NASA scientists use the information collected to study clouds.</u>

Try It

Look at this sample done by an imaginary student named Lakeisha. Analyze Lakeisha's work. Cross out incorrect information. What should she do to score higher?

2. How do students help NASA study clouds? Explain your answer using details from the text.

Lakeisha's Notes: students observe and measure parts of the weather; record clouds, temperature, precipitation during the day

Lakeisha's Answer: Students observe and measure parts of the weather including cloud type, temperature, and precipitation throughout the day while they are at school.

To score higher, Lakeisha needs to _____

Grade 3 Writing Prompt

Read the writing prompt in the box. Write on a separate sheet of paper.

> Describe the forces that change Earth's surface. In your description, include forces that quickly change Earth's surface and forces that slowly change Earth's surface.

The information in the box below will help you remember what you should think about when you write your composition.

> REMEMBER—YOU SHOULD
> ❑ write the main ideas that answer the question about forces that change Earth's surface, including the details that support each idea.
> ❑ present your ideas logically and in an organized way.
> ❑ choose words that say exactly what you want to say.
> ❑ write complete sentences, and make sure that your sentences are varied.
> ❑ check for correct spelling, grammar, punctuation, and word usage.

© Pearson Education, Inc.

Classifying Trash

Your assignment is to prepare a television news report describing how everyone can reduce, reuse, and recycle.

Station 1

Use the card at the station to correctly set up the equipment.

Trash Classification

Decide which items in the bag of trash could be reused, recycled, or used as mulch. List the items in each category.

_____

_____

_____

Station 2

Use the card at the station to correctly set up the equipment.

Trash Measurement

Find the mass of the entire bag of trash. Then sort the trash into three piles: recyclable, not recyclable, and plant material. Find the mass of each pile.

Masses			
Total	Recyclable	Not Recyclable	Plant Material

Station 3

Use the card at the station to correctly set up the equipment.

Reuse Suggestions

For three items you classified as reusable or recyclable, describe a way that each item could be reused.

_____

_____

_____

_____

Data Analysis

You have completed your study of the trash. Use the data you have collected and what you know about conservation to answer the following questions.

What would you say on the television news report about ways to reduce, reuse, and recycle trash? What would you say about using plant materials to make compost?

_____

_____

_____

_____

_____

Read each question and choose the best answer.
Then fill in the circle next to the correct answer.

❶ Which of the following **best** describes matter?

Ⓐ anything that is made of only one element

Ⓑ anything that takes up space and has mass

Ⓒ anything that is found on the periodic table

Ⓓ anything that you can observe with your senses

❷ A scientist describes an object as small, shiny, and bumpy. The scientist is observing the object's _____.

Ⓕ senses

Ⓖ density

Ⓗ volume

Ⓘ properties

❸ What type of matter is made of particles that are tightly packed together and firmly connected?

Ⓐ gas

Ⓑ solid

Ⓒ liquid

Ⓓ plasma

❹ How is a gas different from a solid or liquid?

Ⓕ A gas has a certain shape that does not change.

Ⓖ A gas changes shape over a long period of time.

Ⓗ A gas spreads out to fill whatever space is available.

Ⓘ A gas has a tightly packed shape, but jiggles very quickly.

5 How are elements organized in the periodic table?

Ⓐ They are organized by their individual shapes.

Ⓑ They are organized by the mass of each element.

Ⓒ They are organized by their individual properties.

Ⓓ They are organized by the volume of each element.

6 Which choice below **best** completes the sentence?

_____ is the smallest particle of an element that has the properties of that element.

Ⓕ a solid

Ⓖ a gram

Ⓗ an atom

Ⓘ an ounce

7 Look at the illustration below.

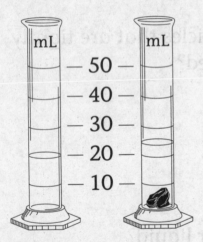

What is the volume of the rock?

Ⓐ 1 mL

Ⓑ 5 mL

Ⓒ 25 mL

Ⓓ You cannot tell from the picture.

8 How is mass different from weight?

Ⓕ Mass is different in different places.

Ⓖ Mass is measured in ounces and pounds.

Ⓗ Mass changes from Earth to the Moon.

Ⓘ Mass remains the same no matter where the object is.

9 A golfer hits a ball into a pond. The ball sinks in the pond. What does this tell the golfer about the golf ball?

Ⓐ The golf ball had little buoyancy.

Ⓑ The golf ball had a lot of buoyancy.

Ⓒ The golf ball is less dense than the water.

Ⓓ The golf ball must have had cork in the middle.

10 Which of the following is **best** measured with kilometers?

Ⓕ the length of a pencil

Ⓖ the height of a student

Ⓗ the length of a classroom

Ⓘ the distance from one city to another

11 How can you measure the volume of a box?

Ⓐ Use a balance.

Ⓑ See how many cubes of a known size fit inside the box.

Ⓒ Use a hand lens to see the small markings on a metric ruler.

Ⓓ Compare the mass of the box with the mass of a standard box of the same size.

Write the answer to the question on the lines.

12 Look at the illustration below.

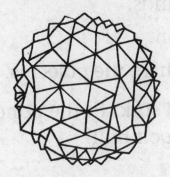

Describe the object's properties. Tell about a tool you could use to observe the object in more detail. (2 points)

_____

_____

_____

Write the answers to the question on a separate sheet of paper.

13 A student finds a small, unknown object during a recent scientific dig.

Part A Explain how the student can find the mass of the object. Include in your answer the units used to record the mass.

Part B Describe how the student can find the volume of the object. Include in your answer the units used to record the volume. (4 points)

**Read each question and choose the best answer.
Then fill in the circle next to the correct answer.**

1 Which of the following is a physical change?

Ⓐ cutting fruit

Ⓑ cooking eggs

Ⓒ rusting metal

Ⓓ burning wood

2 Choose the words that belong in the sentence.
When water changes from a liquid to a solid, it _____,
which is a _____ change.

Ⓕ melts, physical

Ⓖ melts, chemical

Ⓗ freezes, physical

Ⓘ freezes, chemical

3 Why is lemonade a solution?

Ⓐ It is one substance whose kind of matter is changed.

Ⓑ It is one substance whose kind of matter is not changed.

Ⓒ It is a combination of two or more substances and a
new kind of matter is made.

Ⓓ It is a combination of two or more substances and the
kind of matter of each is not changed.

4 Look at the illustration below. Complete the sentence.

This tossed salad is an example of a

Ⓕ mixture.

Ⓖ solution.

Ⓗ melted substance.

Ⓘ chemical change.

5 How can you separate a saltwater mixture?

Ⓐ Boil it.

Ⓑ Freeze it.

Ⓒ Add food coloring.

Ⓓ Pour it through a strainer.

6 Why is baking cookie batter a chemical change?

Ⓕ The substances that make up the batter are heated.

Ⓖ The substances that make up the batter can be separated easily.

Ⓗ The substances that make up the batter change the way they look.

Ⓘ The substances that make up the batter become a different kind of matter.

7 Look at the illustration below.

Which of the following **best** describes what the sculptor is doing to the rock?

Ⓐ He is causing a physical change.

Ⓑ He is causing a chemical change.

Ⓒ He is not causing a physical or a chemical change.

Ⓓ He is causing both a physical and a chemical change.

8 Which of the following is a chemical change?

Ⓕ frying eggs

Ⓖ ripping paper

Ⓗ freezing water

Ⓘ making lemonade

9 How is a chemical change different from a physical change?

Ⓐ A physical change produces new kinds of matter.

Ⓑ A chemical change produces new kinds of matter.

Ⓒ A physical change occurs at much lower temperatures.

Ⓓ A chemical change occurs much more slowly than a physical change does.

© Pearson Education, Inc.

Write the answers to the questions on the lines.

❿ Identify four ways that physical changes can occur in matter. (2 points)

_____

_____

_____

⓫ Explain how chemical changes help you use a battery-operated cell phone. (2 points)

_____

_____

_____

Write the answer to the question on a separate sheet of paper.

⓬ How are mixtures and solutions similar? How are they different? Give examples. (4 points)

**Read each question and choose the best answer.
Then fill in the circle next to the correct answer.**

1 How would you best describe the motion of a Ferris wheel?

Ⓐ wave

Ⓑ circular

Ⓒ forward

Ⓓ backward

2 Choose the words that belong in the sentence.

If a stoplight is in front of the car and then behind the car, the _____ of the stoplight has changed.

Ⓕ relative motion

Ⓖ circular motion

Ⓗ relative position

Ⓘ circular position

3 A bicyclist travels at 8 mph, 12 mph, 9 mph, and 15 mph. How can you **best** describe the bicyclist's speed?

Ⓐ fast

Ⓑ slow

Ⓒ variable

Ⓓ constant

4 If the same amount of force is applied to each box below, which box will move the greatest distance?

Ⓕ 7 kg box

Ⓖ 12 kg box

Ⓗ 23 kg box

Ⓘ 100 kg box

5 Which surface produces the least amount of friction?

Ⓐ rocky gravel road

Ⓑ grassy soccer field

Ⓒ bumpy new carpet

Ⓓ smooth ceramic tile

6 Look at the illustration below.

Team A   **Team B**

How can Team A win the tug-of-war game?

Ⓕ Team A pulls with a lesser force than Team B.

Ⓖ Team B pulls with a greater force than Team A.

Ⓗ Team A pulls with a greater force than Team B.

Ⓘ Team A and Team B pull with the same amount of force, but Team A players use a looser grip.

7 A pitcher throws a baseball from the mound. As it moves toward the batter it starts to move toward the ground. What force pulls the baseball toward the ground?

Ⓐ gravity

Ⓑ friction

Ⓒ pressure

Ⓓ magnetism

8 Which of the following is an example of work?

Ⓕ kicking a ball downhill

Ⓖ thinking about homework

Ⓗ holding the ball before winding up for a pitch

Ⓘ pushing against a concrete pillar with all your might

9 Which tool is a wedge?

Ⓐ axe

Ⓑ ramp

Ⓒ jar lid

Ⓓ doorknob

10 Look at the illustration below.

Which simple machine raises the flag up the pole?

Ⓕ lever

Ⓖ screw

Ⓗ pulley

Ⓘ wheel and axle

Write the answers to the questions on the lines.

11 Describe two ways gravity can affect the movement of a wheel and axle in a bicycle. (2 points)

_____

_____

_____

_____

12 How do simple machines make work easier? (2 points)

_____

_____

Write your answer to the question on a separate sheet of paper.

13 *Part A* Identify three contact forces and two non-contact forces.

Part B Explain how contact forces are different from non-contact forces. Give examples to support your answer. (4 points)

**Read each question and choose the best answer.
Then fill in the circle next to the correct answer.**

1 Complete the sentence.
The Sun's energy reaches Earth as _____.

    Ⓐ heat energy and light energy

    Ⓑ kinetic energy and light energy

    Ⓒ kinetic energy and chemical energy

    Ⓓ electrical energy and chemical energy

2 What happens when we burn fuels such as coal and gasoline?

    Ⓕ We change heat energy to light energy to do work.

    Ⓖ We change kinetic energy to heat energy to do work.

    Ⓗ We release the potential energy within them to do work.

    Ⓘ We release the electrical energy within them to do work.

3 Which of these objects has kinetic energy?

    Ⓐ car moving on a road

    Ⓑ skier going down a slope

    Ⓒ ball rolling down a ramp

    Ⓓ all of the above.

4 What happens to the chemical energy in the battery when you use an electric toothbrush?

    Ⓕ It changes into kinetic energy and then potential energy.

    Ⓖ It changes into potential energy and then kinetic energy.

    Ⓗ It changes into electrical energy and then kinetic energy.

    Ⓘ It changes into kinetic energy and then electrical energy.

5 What is an electric circuit?

Ⓐ the movement of electric energy

Ⓑ an outlet you can plug a cord into

Ⓒ the path that an electric current flows through

Ⓓ a machine used to change sunlight into electricity

6 What is the trough of a wave?

Ⓕ the top of the wave

Ⓖ the width of the wave

Ⓗ the length of the wave

Ⓘ the bottom of the wave

7 What happens when a warm object comes into contact with a cool object?

Ⓐ The cool object loses heat.

Ⓑ The warm object gains heat.

Ⓒ The warm object loses heat and the cool one gains heat.

Ⓓ The cool object loses heat and the warm one gains heat.

8 When can you notice friction?

Ⓕ when wood burns

Ⓖ when sunlight warms the sand at a beach

Ⓗ when you heat frozen vegetables in a pot on the stove

Ⓘ when you warm your hands by rubbing them together

9 How does heat make liquid water change?

    Ⓐ The liquid water becomes ice.

    Ⓑ The liquid water becomes a solid.

    Ⓒ The liquid water evaporates and disappears.

    Ⓓ The liquid water evaporates and becomes a gas.

10 What is a chemical change that gives off light and heat?

    Ⓕ boiling

    Ⓖ burning

    Ⓗ freezing

    Ⓘ evaporating

11 Look at the illustration.

What causes a shadow like the one in the picture?

    Ⓐ The path of light is blocked by the puppet.

    Ⓑ Light reflects off the puppet onto a surface.

    Ⓒ The path of light bends around the puppet.

    Ⓓ Light is refracted as it moves through the puppet.

12 How does the lens in a telescope make objects appear larger?

 Ⓕ It reflects light.

 Ⓖ It refracts light.

 Ⓗ It absorbs light.

 Ⓘ It separates light.

Write the answers to the questions on the lines.

13 Why will paper stick to a balloon that you have rubbed on your hair? (2 points)

_____

_____

_____

14 What are two ways that energy can travel from one place to another? (2 points)

_____

_____

Write your answer to the question on a separate sheet of paper.

15 Name three main sources of light and give examples of each. (4 points)

**Read each question and choose the best answer.
Then fill in the circle next to the correct answer.**

1 Which of the following is true about sound?

Ⓐ All sounds are loud.

Ⓑ All sounds are made when matter moves.

Ⓒ Some sounds are so loud you cannot hear them.

Ⓓ Some sounds are made when matter moves and some
are made when matter rests.

2 Matter moving back and forth quickly is called

Ⓕ pitch.

Ⓖ vibration.

Ⓗ a soft sound.

Ⓘ a loud sound.

3 Hitting a tambourine with less force will make the sound

Ⓐ softer.

Ⓑ louder.

Ⓒ higher in pitch.

Ⓓ higher in vibration.

4 How do wind instruments make sound?

Ⓕ Air inside them vibrates.

Ⓖ Reeds inside them vibrate.

Ⓗ Someone hits the instrument.

Ⓘ Someone presses valves on the instrument.

5 Look at the illustration below.

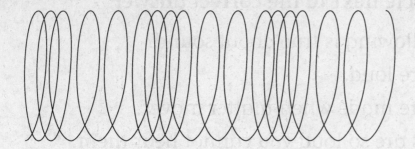

Which type of wave is shown in the picture?

Ⓐ travel wave

Ⓑ particle wave

Ⓒ contraction wave

Ⓓ compression wave

6 Why does sound usually travel most slowly through gases?

Ⓕ The particles in gases are larger than the particles in liquids and solids.

Ⓖ The particles in gases are smaller than the particles in liquids and solids.

Ⓗ The particles in gases are closer together than the particles in liquids and solids.

Ⓘ The particles in gases are farther apart than the particles in liquids and solids.

7 Which part of the ear has a shell-shaped part filled with liquid?

Ⓐ the eardrum

Ⓑ the inner ear

Ⓒ the outer ear

Ⓓ the little bones

8 Look at the illustration below.

Choose the words that belong in the sentence.

The instrument shown above is a _____, which is a type of _____ instrument.

   Ⓕ clarinet, wind

   Ⓖ saxophone, wind

   Ⓗ clarinet, percussion

   Ⓘ saxophone, percussion

9 The same sound travels through air, water, milk, and steel. Through which matter will the sound travel most quickly?

   Ⓐ air

   Ⓑ milk

   Ⓒ water

   Ⓓ steel

10 How is the length of a sound wave measured?

   Ⓕ from the beginning of the wave to the end of the wave

   Ⓖ from the beginning of the wave to half way through the wave

   Ⓗ from the center of one compression to the center of the next compression

   Ⓘ from the end of one compression to the beginning of the next compression

Write the answers to the questions on the lines.

⓫ A student says that an object that vibrates more quickly has a lower pitch. Is the student correct? Explain your reasoning. (2 points)

_____

_____

_____

_____

⓬ Sound travels in waves. Compare the speeds at which sound waves travel as they go through air, water, and solids. Also explain why the speeds are different. (2 points)

_____

_____

_____

_____

_____

Write your answer to the question on a separate sheet of paper.

⓭ Describe how sound waves travel through human ears to the brain. (4 points)

**Read each question and choose the best answer.
Then fill in the circle next to the correct answer.**

1 A student pours 25 mL of water into a graduated cylinder.
She then placed an object in the cylinder. She now reads
the volume as 42 mL. What is the volume of the object?

Ⓐ 17 mL   Ⓒ 42 mL

Ⓑ 25 mL   Ⓓ 67 mL

2 Four containers sit on a shelf. Which one contains a
solution?

Ⓕ the container with water in it

Ⓖ the container with a rusty nail in it

Ⓗ the container with lemonade in it

Ⓘ the container with rocks and dirt in it

3 A golfer hits a golf ball so that it flies high into the air.
What force brings the golf ball back to the ground?

Ⓐ gravity

Ⓑ friction

Ⓒ magnetism

Ⓓ atmospheric pressure

4 Two objects have the same volume. What measurement
should you make to find out which object has the greater
density?

Ⓕ area

Ⓖ mass

Ⓗ length

Ⓘ perimeter

5 Look at the illustration below.

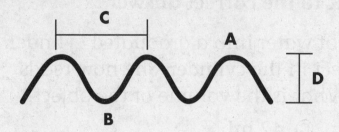

Which letter points to the crest of the wave?

Ⓐ A

Ⓑ B

Ⓒ C

Ⓓ D

6 A girl makes a cup of hot chocolate, but the hot chocolate is too hot. She places an ice cube in the cup. Which of the following **best** describes what happens when the hot chocolate comes in contact with the ice cube?

Ⓕ The ice cube loses heat.

Ⓖ The hot chocolate gains heat.

Ⓗ The hot chocolate loses heat and the ice cube gains heat.

Ⓘ The ice cube loses heat and the hot chocolate gains heat.

7 A man makes a noise in different locations. In which location will the sound from his noise travel the fastest?

Ⓐ The sound will travel fastest down a long hallway.

Ⓑ The sound will travel fastest through a pool of water.

Ⓒ The sound will travel fastest through a solid metal rod.

Ⓓ The sound will travel fastest from one side of a room to another.

8 Look at the illustration.
What is happening to the wood in this picture?

Ⓕ It is undergoing a heat change from wood
to ash.

Ⓖ It is undergoing a phase change from wood
to ash.

Ⓗ It is undergoing a physical change from wood to ash.

Ⓘ It is undergoing a chemical change from wood to ash.

9 When you use a doorknob to open a door, what simple
machine are you using?

Ⓐ lever

Ⓒ wedge

Ⓑ pulley

Ⓓ wheel and axle

10 Four students make 4 different racing cars. To start the
cars, each student pushes each car with the same amount
of force. Which car will have the greatest speed?

Ⓕ A 25 kilogram car moving across the grass.

Ⓖ A 55 kilogram car moving across the grass.

Ⓗ A 25 kilogram car moving along a paved road.

Ⓘ A 55 kilogram car moving along a paved road.

11 A rider stands on a skateboard at the top of a hill. What
happens when the rider starts to go down the hill?

Ⓐ The skateboard's kinetic energy decreases.

Ⓑ The skateboard's potential energy increases.

Ⓒ The skateboard's potential energy changes to kinetic
energy.

Ⓓ The skateboard's kinetic energy changes to potential
energy.

Write the answers to the questions on the lines.

12 Water can undergo physical changes when its temperature changes. Describe the types of physical changes water can undergo and explain what causes the changes. (2 points)

_____

_____

_____

_____

13 Two students are using drums to make sound. Explain how the students are making sound and then explain how the students could make both soft and loud sounds. (2 points)

_____

_____

_____

_____

Write your answer to the question on a separate sheet of paper.

14 Matter is all around us.

Part A Tell what matter is, what three forms it takes, and what it is made of.

Part B Tell the difference between an element and an atom. (4 points)

Exercising in Space

Directions: Read about the importance of exercise for astronauts while in space. Then follow the directions on pages 90–95.

Do you like to exercise? Running, playing ball, and bicycling are exercises that have motion, speed, and force. But you don't have to be moving to exercise your muscles. Pushing against a wall may not do any work, but the pushing force you use exercises your muscles.

On Earth, the force of gravity helps you exercise. That's because every time you lift your legs or arms, you have to lift them against the force of gravity. So, you have to give your arms and legs force, and that's good exercise. Suppose you are an astronaut aboard the Space Shuttle or the International Space Station. You do not feel the tug of gravity. The very high speed it takes to stay in orbit around Earth is the reason. It reduces the effect of gravity to zero. You float around the cabin. This makes exercising in space harder than on Earth. Imagine trying to push against a wall on the shuttle. It just sends you off in another direction!

Without exercise, your muscles and bones get weaker. Astronauts in space must exercise every day to keep their muscles and bones healthy.

Special exercise machines had to be built for space. One kind of machine is like an exercise bicycle. Another machine is like a treadmill. The third kind of machine is like a rowing machine that pushes and pulls on muscles. Astronauts have to be strapped to the machines so they don't float away. Then they put on weights so they can exercise their muscles.

Information learned about muscles and bones in space has helped people on Earth know more about keeping healthy. Many gyms on Earth have exercise machines based on those designed for space. This is just another example of how space-age technology helps everyone.

© Pearson Education, Inc.

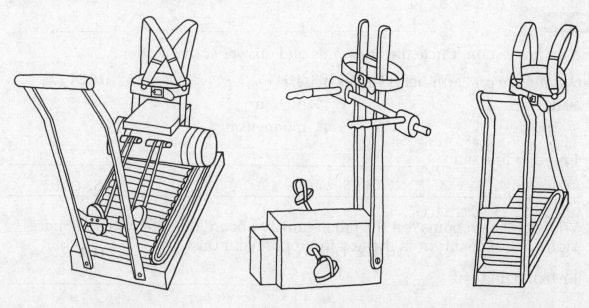

Strategy 1 Locate Key Words in the Question

Directions: Before you can answer a question, you need to understand it. Follow these steps to understand the question.

- Read the question.
- Ask yourself: "**Who** or **what** is the question about?" Words that tell "who" or "what" are **key words**. Circle key words.
- Look for and circle other key words. Often question words and other important words are key words.
- Turn the question into a statement using key words. Follow this model: "I need to find out _____."

Learn

Read the question. Circle the key words and then complete the sentence.

1. (Why) must (astronauts exercise every day) while they are in (space)?

   - Turn the question into a statement using key words.

   Ⓐ It lets them adjust better to life in space.
   Ⓑ It allows them to feel the pull of gravity.
   Ⓒ It helps keep bones and muscles healthy.
   Ⓓ It prevents them from becoming sick in space.

   I need to find out _why astronauts exercise every day._

Try It

Read each question. Circle the key words and answer each question.

2. What force on Earth helps you exercise?
   Ⓐ inertia   Ⓒ friction
   Ⓑ gravity   Ⓓ magnetism

   I need to find out _____

   _____

3. Why don't astronauts feel the tug of gravity aboard the International Space Station? Use details from the text to support your answer.

   I need to find out _____

   _____

Name _____

Strategy 2 Locate Key Words in the Text

Directions: You can also understand a question by thinking about where you need to look for the answer. Follow these steps to understand the question.

- Read the question.
- Look for and **circle key words** in the question.
- Look for and circle key words in the text that match key words in the question. Decide where to look for the answer.
  - To find the answer, you may have to **look in one place in the text**. The answer is *right there* in the text.
  - To find the answer, you may have to **look in several places in the text**. You have to *think* and *search* for information.
  - To find the answer, you may have to **combine what you know with what the author tells you**. The answer comes from the *author* and *you*.

Learn

Read the question. Circle the key words and then complete the sentence.

1. (Why) must (astronauts exercise every day) while they are in (space)?

   I found the answer in *paragraph 3, sentence 2.*

- Look for and circle key words in the question.
- Look for and circle key words in the text that match key words in the question.

Try It

Read each question. Circle the key words and answer the question.

- The question asks why astronauts must exercise in space.
- You will have to look in one place in the text for information.

2. What force on Earth helps you exercise?

   Ⓐ inertia

   Ⓑ gravity

   Ⓒ friction

   Ⓓ magnetism

   I found the answer in _____

   _____

3. Why don't astronauts feel the tug of gravity aboard the International Space Station? Use details from the text to support your answer.

   I found the answer in _____

Strategy 3 Choose the Right Answer

Directions: Use this strategy for a multiple-choice question for which you are not positive of the right answer.

- Read the question.
- Read each answer choice.
- **Rule out** any choice you know is wrong. Go back to the text to rule out other choices.
- Mark your answer choice.
- **Check your answer** by comparing it with the text.

Learn

Cross out any choice you know is wrong. Next, go back to the text to rule out any other choices. Then mark your choice.

1. Why must astronauts exercise every day while they are in space?
   - Ⓐ ~~It lets them adjust better to life in space.~~
   - Ⓑ ~~It allows them to feel the pull of gravity.~~
   - Ⓒ It helps keep bones and muscles healthy.
   - Ⓓ ~~It prevents them from becoming sick in space.~~

- Look for this subject in the text.

- Rule out incorrect choices. Choose answer C because the text supports this choice.

Try It

Cross out any choice you know is wrong. Next, go back to the text to rule out any other choices. Then mark your answer.

2. What force on Earth helps you exercise?
   - Ⓕ inertia
   - Ⓖ gravity
   - Ⓗ friction
   - Ⓘ magnetism

3. Why don't astronauts feel the tug of gravity aboard the International Space Station?
   - Ⓐ There is no gravity out of Earth's atmosphere.
   - Ⓑ The high speed of the space station reduces gravity's effect.
   - Ⓒ The International Space Station is made of gravity-resistant material.
   - Ⓓ The pull of gravity from the Sun overpowers the pull of Earth's gravity.

© Pearson Education, Inc.

Assessment Book

Name _____

Strategy 4 # Use Information from the Text

Directions: A question may ask you to support your answer with details from the text. If it does, then you must include information from the text. Follow these steps to understand questions like this.

- Read the question.
- Look for and circle key words in the question.
- **Make notes** about details from the text that answer the question.
- Reread the question and your notes.
- If details are missing, go back to the text.

Learn

Use information from the text to answer the question.

1. (How) has (information learned) about (muscles) and (bones) in (space) (helped people) on (Earth?) Use details from the text to support your answer.

   My Notes: _gyms have machines based on those designed for space, people know more about keeping healthy_

   My Answer: _People on Earth have learned how to stay healthier from the information learned in space. Gyms also have equipment that is similar to the special machines made for exercising in space._

- Circle key words in the question. The question asks you how information about muscles and bones learned in space helps people on Earth.

- Read text and make notes about how people on Earth use the information about muscles and bones learned in space.

Try It

2. What types of exercise machines are used by astronauts in space?

   My Notes: _____

   _____

   _____

   My Answer: _____

   _____

   _____

© Pearson Education, Inc.

Assessment Book

Unit C Test Talk **93**

Strategy 5 Use Information from Graphics

Directions: A question may ask you about graphics or ask you to support your answer with details from graphics. If it does, you must include information from the graphics. Follow these instructions to answer questions about graphics.

- Read the question.
- Look for and circle key words in the question.
- Use what you know to analyze the graphic.
- Use details from the graph to answer the question.

Learn

Look at the picture on page 89. Use information from this picture to answer the question.

1. Based on the (picture,)(how) is the (way astronauts) (use exercise equipment different) from how the equipment is used on (Earth)? Use details to support your answer.

> - Look for and circle key words in the question.

To find the answer, I will <u>look at the picture and see how exercise equipment</u>

<u>is different for astronauts than for people on Earth.</u>

My Answer: <u>The astronauts use similar machines, but there are straps on</u>

<u>the machines so they do not float away.</u>

Try It

Look at the picture on page 89. Use information from the picture to answer the question.

2. Based on the picture, what are some types of exercise equipment used by astronauts in space? Use details to support your answer.

To find the answer, I will _____

_____

My Answer: _____

_____

_____

_____

Strategy 6 Write Your Answer to Score High

Directions: A question may ask you to write an answer. Follow these steps to write a correct, complete, and focused answer.

Learn

Look at this sample written by an imaginary student named Mike. Analyze Mike's work. Cross out incorrect information. What should he do to score higher?

1. (How) does the (force) of (gravity) help you (exercise)? Use details from the text to support your answer.

   > • Mike circled words in the question.

   Mike's Notes: lift legs or arms against the force of gravity; pushing against a wall exercises muscles; give arms and legs force and that is good exercise; ~~gravity makes exercises easier to perform~~

   > • Mike's notes have errors.

   Mike's Answer: The force of gravity helps you exercise because when you lift your arms or legs, you have to lift them against the force of gravity, which makes it easier to lift your arms or legs. Gravity also helps work your muscles and bones when you push against a wall.

   > • Mike's answer has information that is incorrect and incomplete.

   To score higher, Mike needs to <u>delete the information about gravity making exercise easier and replace it with a sentence about gravity making it harder to lift your arms and legs.</u>

Try It

Look at this sample done by an imaginary student named Kay. Analyze Kay's work. Cross out incorrect information. What should she do to score higher?

2. Why is exercising in space harder than exercising on Earth? Explain your answer using details from the text.

   Kay's Notes: exercising is more difficult, no gravity, different machines, must be strapped in, pushing against a wall moves you in another direction

   Kay's Answer: Exercising in space is harder than exercising on Earth because there is no gravity or gyms in space. Astronauts have to use special machines to workout that are very different from the machines on Earth.

   To score higher, Kay needs to _____

   _____

Grade 3 Writing Prompt

Read the writing prompt in this box. Write on a separate sheet of paper.

> Write a letter to explain what physical and chemical changes are to another student in your grade. Include an example of each type of change.

The information in the box below will help you remember what you should think about when you write your composition.

> REMEMBER—YOU SHOULD
> - ❑ write the main ideas that will explain what physical and chemical changes are and how they are different from each other, including the details that support each idea.
> - ❑ present your ideas logically and in an organized way.
> - ❑ choose words that say exactly what you want to say.
> - ❑ write complete sentences, and make sure that your sentences are varied.
> - ❑ check for correct spelling, grammar, punctuation, and word usage.

© Pearson Education, Inc.

Investigating Physical Properties

Investigate the objects in the stations. Use their physical properties to describe them.

Station 1

Use the card at the station to correctly set up the equipment.

Strings

Record the lengths of the strings in the table. List three physical properties that describe each string.

String	Length	Description
A		
B		
C		

Station 2

Use the card at the station to correctly set up the equipment.

Beans

Classify the beans into three groups. Put the groups into the bags labeled "A," "B," or "C."

Record the mass of each bean group in the table. List three physical properties that describe each group.

Group	Mass	Description
A		
B		
C		

Station 3

Use the card at the station to correctly set up the equipment.

Objects

Use the magnet to help investigate the objects. Divide the objects into two groups based on your investigation. Describe the two groups.

Group	Items	Description
1		
2		

Data Analysis

Now you have classified and measured all of the objects. Think about the physical properties of the items and use what you know to answer the following questions.

How could you make a physical change in the strings?

_____

_____

How could you make a physical change in the beans?

_____

_____

How could you make a physical change in the paper clips?

_____

_____

_____

**Read each question and choose the best answer.
Then fill in the circle next to the correct answer.**

1 Earth spins around an imaginary line called the

Ⓐ axis.

Ⓑ eclipse.

Ⓒ horizon.

Ⓓ rotation.

2 How long does it take for Earth to rotate one time?

Ⓕ about 24 days

Ⓖ about one year

Ⓗ about 24 hours

Ⓘ about one week

3 What causes shade beneath a tree?

Ⓐ the seasons

Ⓑ the phases of the Moon

Ⓒ the tree blocking sunlight

Ⓓ Earth reflecting sunlight

4 Shadows cast by the Sun are the shortest

Ⓕ at noon.

Ⓖ at night.

Ⓗ in the morning.

Ⓘ in the afternoon.

5 The northern half of Earth tilts away from the Sun during which month below?

Ⓐ June

Ⓑ March

Ⓒ December

Ⓓ September

6 What causes the seasons to change on Earth?

Ⓕ the tilt of Earth and its rotation

Ⓖ the tilt of the Sun and its rotation

Ⓗ the tilt of Earth and its revolution around the Sun

Ⓘ the tilt of the Sun and its revolution around Earth

7 Complete the sentence.
In the summer, the number of hours of daylight is
_____ the number of hours of darkness.

Ⓐ less than

Ⓑ the same as

Ⓒ greater than

Ⓓ about equal to

8 How long does it take the Moon to go once around Earth?

Ⓕ longer than the four seasons put together

Ⓖ longer than it takes Earth to go around the Sun

Ⓗ about as long as it takes Earth to rotate once on its axis

Ⓘ about as long as it takes the Moon to rotate once on its axis

9 Look at the illustration.

What is this phase of the Moon called?

Ⓐ a full Moon

Ⓑ a new Moon

Ⓒ a crescent Moon

Ⓓ a first quarter Moon

10 Use the illustration to answer the question.

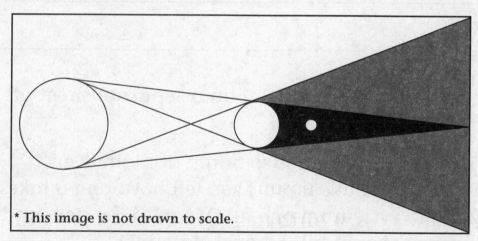

* This image is not drawn to scale.

What causes a lunar eclipse like the one shown in the picture?

Ⓕ Earth casts a shadow on the Sun.

Ⓖ Earth casts a shadow on the Moon.

Ⓗ The Moon casts a shadow on Earth.

Ⓘ The Sun casts a shadow on the Moon.

11 Why do some stars appear dimmer than others?

Ⓐ They are bigger than other stars.

Ⓑ They are hotter than other stars.

Ⓒ They are closer to Earth than other stars.

Ⓓ They are farther away from Earth than other stars.

Write the answers to the questions on the lines.

12 What would Earth be like without the Sun? (2 points)

_____

_____

13 If you observe constellations at different times of the year, what will you notice about how they move? (2 points)

_____

_____

Write your answer to the question on a separate sheet of paper.

14 Explain why the full Moon is so bright at night even though it does not make light. Then tell how long it takes for the Moon to cycle from one full Moon to the next and what happens between full Moons. (4 points)

Name _____

Read each question and choose the best answer.
Then fill in the circle next to the correct answer.

1 The Sun is

Ⓐ a star.

Ⓑ a comet.

Ⓒ a planet.

Ⓓ an asteroid.

2 Which of these planets is the farthest from the Sun?

Ⓕ Venus

Ⓖ Saturn

Ⓗ Mercury

Ⓘ Neptune

3 Why is Mercury very dry and hot?

Ⓐ Mercury is the smallest planet.

Ⓑ Mercury is the closest planet to the Sun.

Ⓒ Mercury has a reddish surface that holds in the heat.

Ⓓ Mercury has a thick atmosphere that holds in the heat.

4 A scientist describes a planet in this way: This planet is an inner planet with two moons. The planet has a reddish-orange rocky surface.
Which planet is the scientist describing?

Ⓕ Mars

Ⓖ Earth

Ⓗ Venus

Ⓘ Mercury

© Pearson Education, Inc.

Chapter 16 Test **103**

Chapter 16 Test

5 Look at the illustration below.

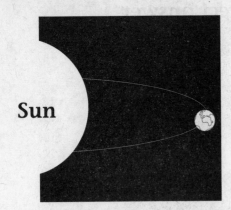

Sun

What is the path shown in the picture?

Ⓐ the rotation of a planet around the Sun

Ⓑ the revolution of the Sun around a planet

Ⓒ the orbit of a planet as it rotates on its axis

Ⓓ the orbit of a planet as it revolves around the Sun

6 Choose the words that belong in the sentence.
The _____ is actually a huge storm on Jupiter that is always there.

Ⓕ Great Breeze

Ⓖ Time Tunnel

Ⓗ Great Red Spot

Ⓘ Man on the Moon

7 Which planet is an inner planet?

Ⓐ Mars

Ⓑ Jupiter

Ⓒ Uranus

Ⓓ Neptune

8 Look at the illustration below.

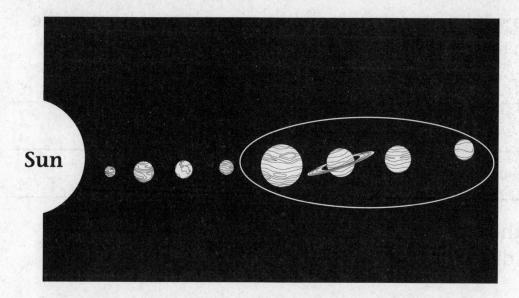

Sun

What do the circled planets have in common?

Ⓕ They all have surfaces that support life.

Ⓖ They all have surfaces that are not solid.

Ⓗ They all have surfaces that are made of rock.

Ⓘ They all have surfaces that have liquid water.

9 Which statement about the four outer planets is true?

Ⓐ They are made of gas.

Ⓑ They all have rings that are easy to see.

Ⓒ They are made of rock.

Ⓓ They all have one moon.

10 What are three features that make the variety of living things on Earth possible?

Ⓕ thick clouds, a lot of heat, and liquid water

Ⓖ liquid water, mild temperatures, and thick clouds

Ⓗ the atmosphere, a lot of heat, and a rocky surface

Ⓘ the atmosphere, mild temperatures, and liquid water

Write the answers to the questions on the lines.

11 Explain why many stars look like pinpoints of light while the Sun seems very big and bright. (2 points)

_____

_____

_____

12 Name the four outer planets and explain which one rotates different from the other three planets. (2 points)

_____

_____

_____

_____

Write your answer to the question on a separate sheet of paper.

13 The inner planets are closest to the Sun in our solar system.

Part A Name the four inner planets and describe a feature of each planet.

Part B List the order of the inner planets starting from the planet closest to the Sun.
(4 points)

**Read each question and choose the best answer.
Then fill in the circle next to the correct answer.**

1 Which answer **best** completes the sentence?
Technology is _____.

Ⓐ the study of computers

Ⓑ a science the Romans invented

Ⓒ asking a question about how the world works

Ⓓ using knowledge to design a new way to do things

2 How do a heating system and an electrical system work
together in a house?

Ⓕ The heating system turns the electrical system on and
off.

Ⓖ The electrical system turns the heating system on and
off.

Ⓗ The heating system burns fuels to operate the electrical
system.

Ⓘ The electrical system burns fuels to operate the heating
system.

3 What invention did Percy Spencer develop after a
chocolate bar melted in his pocket near a radar tube?

Ⓐ the microwave oven

Ⓑ the convection oven

Ⓒ the drip coffee maker

Ⓓ the outdoor propane grill

4 Look at the illustration below.

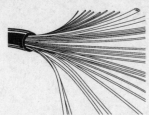

Why are fibers, such as those you see in the picture, replacing standard wires in computer, telephone, and cable television systems?

F The fibers shown do not get hot and can better scramble signals.

G The fibers shown release more heat energy and can better scramble signals.

H The fibers shown do not get hot and can carry more information than standard wires can.

I The fibers shown release more heat energy and can carry more information than standard wires can.

5 Which sentence is true about fuels used to generate electricity?

A The fuels can pollute the air.

B The fuels were invented in Rome.

C The fuels are renewable resources.

D The fuels are called the greatest wonder of the world.

6 In the future, we may use which two renewable resources to meet our energy needs?

F wind energy and coal

G fossil fuels and natural gas

H natural gas and solar energy

I wind energy and solar energy

7 In 312 B.C., Rome completed its first aqueducts. What did the aqueducts bring to Roman cities?

Ⓐ water

Ⓑ electricity

Ⓒ medical care

Ⓓ safer food supplies

8 What two types of technology use a beam of light to read stored information?

Ⓕ CDs and DVDs

Ⓖ VCR tapes and DVDs

Ⓗ audio cassettes and CDs

Ⓘ VCR tapes and audio cassettes

9 Look at the illustration below.

The panels on top of the house are using solar energy to make

Ⓐ fuel.

Ⓑ hot water.

Ⓒ nuclear energy.

Ⓓ hydroelectric power.

10 What is a negative thing about wind and water power?

Ⓕ They are both renewable resources.

Ⓖ They are both nonrenewable resources.

Ⓗ They are both only available along a river.

Ⓘ They both don't supply enough power for our needs.

Write the answers to the questions on the lines.

⓫ Identify two ways technology has changed the kitchen from the 1800s to today. (2 points)

_____

_____

_____

_____

⓬ Why do some people call the National Highway System the greatest wonder of the modern world? (2 points)

_____

_____

_____

_____

Write your answer to the question on a separate sheet of paper.

⓭ Water has been used for many years to generate power.

Part A Explain how water power is used in the modern age.

Part B Identify the positive and negative effects of using modern water power.
(4 points)

© Pearson Education, Inc.

**Read each question and choose the best answer.
Then fill in the circle next to the correct answer.**

1 Why do stars look so small?

Ⓐ They are very far away.

Ⓑ They do not give off much light.

Ⓒ They are all much smaller than our Sun.

Ⓓ They are so crowded in space they can't take up much room.

2 Which of the following occurs about once every $29\frac{1}{2}$ days?

Ⓕ a new Moon

Ⓖ a solar eclipse

Ⓗ a phase Moon

Ⓘ a lunar eclipse

3 Choose the words that **best** complete the sentence.

Earth rotates on its _____ once every _____.

Ⓐ axis, 24 hours

Ⓑ axis, 365 days

Ⓒ orbit, 24 hours

Ⓓ orbit, 365 days

4 During the month of June, what position is Earth in?

Ⓕ The South Pole points directly down.

Ⓖ The South Pole points directly toward the Sun.

Ⓗ The northern half of Earth tilts more toward the Sun.

Ⓘ The northern half of Earth tilts more away from the Sun.

5 Look at the illustration below.

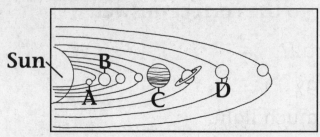

Which of these planets is an inner planet with a thick atmosphere and no moons?

Ⓐ A

Ⓑ B

Ⓒ C

Ⓓ D

6 Which of the following is true about the Sun?

Ⓕ The Sun is a star that is the main source of energy for Earth.

Ⓖ The Sun is a planet that is the main source of energy for Earth.

Ⓗ The Sun is a star that provides a small amount of energy for Earth.

Ⓘ The Sun is a planet that provides a small amount of energy for Earth.

7 A clue for a trivia game is: "This planet is a gas giant covered with thick layers of clouds. For years we've watched a huge storm on this planet and called it the Great Red Spot." What is the answer?

Ⓐ Venus

Ⓑ Saturn

Ⓒ Jupiter

Ⓓ Uranus

8 Look at the illustration below.

The Romans invented the arches shown above to help solve two problems. What did the Romans mainly use the arches for?

Ⓕ building bridges and carrying water

Ⓖ building bridges and building buildings

Ⓗ making monuments and carrying water

Ⓘ making monuments and building buildings

9 Which outer planet is **larger** than the other outer planets?

Ⓐ Jupiter

Ⓑ Saturn

Ⓒ Uranus

Ⓓ Neptune

10 Farmers use GPS systems to

Ⓕ water their crops.

Ⓖ predict the weather.

Ⓗ locate crops that need water or fertilizer.

Ⓘ make harvesting crops faster and easier.

11 Which of the following is an invention that stores, processes, and sends information incredibly fast?

Ⓐ radiation

Ⓑ computer

Ⓒ technology

Ⓓ LCD screen

Write the answers to the questions on the lines.

12 Explain what a phase of the Moon is and describe what causes the phases of the Moon. (2 points)

_____

_____

_____

_____

13 We divide the eight planets that orbit the Sun into two groups. Identify the two groups and explain how the groups are divided. (2 points)

_____

_____

_____

_____

Write your answer to the question on a separate sheet of paper.

14 Energy sources are important in our daily lives. However, nonrenewable energy sources need to be replaced with renewable energy sources if we are going to have enough energy in the future. Identify two renewable energy sources that we have already started using. Then describe at least one benefit and one problem for each energy source you identify. (4 points)

The Hubble Space Telescope

Directions: Read about how NASA has used the Hubble Space Telescope to collect information from space. Then follow the directions on pages 116–121.

You can use a telescope to make stars and other objects in space easier to see. Imagine how many stars you could see with a telescope 13.2 meters (43.5 feet) long and 4.2 meters (14 feet) wide. Imagine it weighing 11,000 kilograms (24,000 pounds). You would not be taking it over to a friend's house to look at stars. A telescope this size would not fit in a car, but it did fit in a Space Shuttle.

In 1990, NASA launched the Hubble Space Telescope. The Hubble stays in space about 600 kilometers (375 miles) above Earth. It revolves around Earth every 97 minutes.

The Hubble collects information from space and sends it to scientists on Earth every day. It provides detailed images of Mars and Pluto. It helps scientists understand more about Uranus and Neptune. The Hubble also has helped scientists learn about objects outside our solar system. It provides information about black holes, quasars, and the birth and death of stars.

The Hubble Telescope was made in a way that makes it easy to repair and update. Since it has been launched, astronauts have made missions to the Hubble to keep it working well. During space walks, astronauts have replaced parts that have worn out. Astronauts also have added parts so that the Hubble always has the newest technology. Each servicing mission adds four to five years to the working life of the Hubble.

NASA is even considering sending a robot to update the telescope, without astronauts!

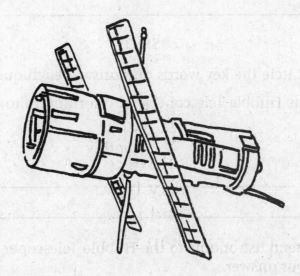

Strategy 1 Locate Key Words in the Question

Directions: Before you can answer a question, you need to understand it. Follow these steps to understand the question.

- Read the question.
- Ask yourself: "**Who** or **what** is the question about?" Words that tell "who" or "what" are **key words**. Circle key words.
- Look for and circle other key words. Often question words and other important words are key words.
- Turn the question into a statement using key words. Follow this model: "I need to find out _____."

Learn

Read the question. Circle the key words and then complete the sentence.

1. (How long) does it (take) the (Hubble Telescope) to (revolve) around (Earth)?

   Ⓐ 28 days   Ⓒ 97 minutes

   Ⓑ 24 hours   Ⓓ 365 days

   > • Turn the question into a statement using key words.

   I need to find out <u>the time it takes the Hubble Telescope to revolve around</u>

   <u>Earth.</u>

Try It

Read each question. Circle the key words and answer each question.

2. How often does the Hubble Telescope send information to Earth?

   Ⓐ daily   Ⓒ yearly

   Ⓑ hourly   Ⓓ monthly

   I need to find out _____

   _____

3. Why does NASA send astronauts to the Hubble Telescope? Use details from the text to support your answer.

   I need to find out _____

   _____

Strategy 2 Locate Key Words in the Text

Directions: You can also understand a question by thinking about where you need to look for the answer. Follow these steps to understand the question.

- Read the question.
- Look for and **circle key words** in the question.
- Look for and circle key words in the text that match key words in the question. Decide where to look for the answer.
  - To find the answer, you may have to **look in one place in the text**. The answer is *right there* in the text.
  - To find the answer, you may have to **look in several places in the text**. You have to *think* and *search* for information.
  - To find the answer, you may have to **combine what you know with what the author tells you**. The answer comes from the *author* and *you*.

Learn

Read the question. Circle the key words and then complete the sentence.

1. How long does it take the Hubble Telescope to revolve around Earth?

   I found the answer in paragraph 2, sentence 3.

- Look for and circle key words in the question.
- Look for and circle key words in the text that match key words in the question.

- The question asks how long it takes the Hubble Telescope to revolve around Earth.
- You will have to look in one place in the text for information.

Try It

Read each question. Circle the key words and answer the question.

2. How often does the Hubble Telescope send information to Earth?

   Ⓐ daily
   Ⓑ hourly
   Ⓒ yearly
   Ⓓ monthly

   I found the answer in _____

   _____

3. Why does NASA send astronauts to the Hubble Telescope? Use details from the text to support your answer.

   I found the answer in _____

   _____

Strategy 3 Choose the Right Answer

Directions: Use this strategy for a multiple-choice question for which you are not positive of the right answer.

- Read the question.
- Read each answer choice.
- **Rule out** any choice you know is wrong. Go back to the text to rule out other choices.
- Mark your answer choice.
- **Check your answer** by comparing it with the text.

Learn

Cross out any choice you know is wrong. Next, go back to the text to rule out any other choices. Then mark your choice.

1. How long does it take the Hubble Telescope to revolve around Earth?

   Ⓐ 28 days
   Ⓑ 24 hours
   Ⓒ 97 minutes
   Ⓓ 365 days

- Look for this subject in the text.

- Rule out incorrect choices. Choose answer C because the text supports this choice.

Try It

Cross out any choice you know is wrong. Next, go back to the text to rule out any other choices. Then mark your answer.

2. How often does the Hubble Telescope send information to Earth?

   Ⓕ daily
   Ⓖ hourly
   Ⓗ yearly
   Ⓘ monthly

3. Why does NASA send astronauts to the Hubble Telescope?

   Ⓐ Astronauts live on the Hubble Telescope.
   Ⓑ Astronauts correct the orbit of the Hubble Telescope.
   Ⓒ Astronauts put new technology on the Hubble Telescope.
   Ⓓ Astronauts download the data from the Hubble Telescope.

© Pearson Education, Inc.

Name _____

Strategy 4 Use Information from the Text

Directions: A question may ask you to support your answer with details from the text. If it does, then you must include information from the text. Follow these steps to understand questions like this.

- Read the question.
- Look for and circle key words in the question.
- **Make notes** about details from the text that answer the question.
- Reread the question and your notes.
- If details are missing, go back to the text.

Learn

Use information from the text to answer the question.

1. (Why) does (NASA send astronauts) to the (Hubble Telescope)? Use details from the text to support your answer.

   My Notes: replaced parts that have worn out, added new parts

   My Answer: Astronauts travel to the Hubble Telescope to replace parts that have worn out. They also travel to the telescope to add new parts so that it always has the newest technology.

- Circle key words in the question. The question asks you why NASA sends astronauts to the Hubble Telescope.

- Read text and make notes about what astronauts do when they travel to the Hubble Telescope.

Try It

2. What objects in space does the Hubble Telescope collect information about for NASA?

   My Notes: _____

   _____

   _____

   My Answer: _____

   _____

   _____

   _____

Strategy 5 Use Information from Graphics

Directions: A question may ask you about graphics or ask you to support your answer with details from graphics. If it does, you must include information from graphics. Follow these instructions to answer questions about graphics.

> - Read the question.
> - Look for and circle key words in the question.
> - Use what you know to analyze the graphics.
> - Use details from the graphics to answer the question.

Learn

Look at the picture on page 115. Use information from this picture to answer the question.

1. Based on the picture, where does the Hubble Telescope get energy from? Use details to support your answer.

   > - Look for and circle key words in the question.

   To find the answer, I will look at the picture that shows the Hubble Telescope and study the telescope and think about what I know about energy sources.

   My Answer: The solar panels on the sides of the Hubble Telescope collect solar energy for the telescope to use in space.

Try It

Look at the picture on page 115. Use information from this picture to answer the question.

2. Based on the picture, how might the Hubble Telescope compare in size to a telescope you might use on Earth? Use details to support your answer.

   To find the answer, I will _____

   _____

   _____

   My Answer: _____

   _____

   _____

Strategy 6 Write Your Answer to Score High

Directions: A question may ask you to write an answer. Make sure to write a correct, complete, and focused answer.

Learn

Look at this sample written by an imaginary student named Ty. Analyze Ty's work. Cross out incorrect information. What should he do to score higher?

1. What information does the Hubble Telescope collect for NASA? Use details from the text to support your answer.

- Ty circled words in the question.

Ty's Notes: info from space; images of Mars and Pluto; ~~atmosphere of Jupiter and Neptune;~~ ~~atmosphere samples from planets;~~ info about black holes and quasars

- Ty's notes have incorrect information.

Ty's Answer: The Hubble Telescope collects information for NASA about space. The Hubble Telescope provides images of Mars and Pluto for scientists. It also collects atmosphere samples from planets such as Jupiter and Neptune and information about black holes and quasars.

- Ty's answer has information that is incorrect and incomplete.

To score higher, Ty needs to delete the information about collecting atmosphere samples since that is not accurate. He could also add information about the birth and death of stars.

Try It

Look at this sample done by an imaginary student named Jack. Analyze Jack's work. Cross out incorrect information. What should he do to score higher?

2. How is the Hubble Telescope different from a telescope you might use in school? Explain your answer using details from the text.

Jack's Notes: bigger, revolves around Earth, can see close-ups of objects

Jacks Answer: The Hubble Telescope is bigger and heavier than a telescope that we would use in school. The Hubble Telescope moves around Earth and sends images to Earth. It takes pictures of objects we can see on Earth.

To score higher, Jack needs to _____

_____

Grade 3 Writing Prompt

Read the writing prompt in the box. Write on a separate sheet of paper.

> Your class is holding a debate about what energy sources scientists should develop for the future. Decide which renewable or nonrenewable resources you think should be developed for the future. Write an argument that explains why the resources you choose have more benefits than the other possibilities.

The information in the box below will help you remember what you should think about when you write your composition.

> REMEMBER—YOU SHOULD
> ❑ write down the types of resources you think should be developed, including the details that support why you chose each resource.
> ❑ present your ideas logically and in an organized way.
> ❑ choose words that say exactly what you want to say.
> ❑ write complete sentences, and make sure that your sentences are varied.
> ❑ check for correct spelling, grammar, punctuation, and word usage.

Name _____

Modeling the Moon's Appearance

Imagine that you must model the phases of the Moon and a lunar eclipse for a class presentation. Your job is to correctly show the appearance of the Moon using a model.

Station 1

Use the card at the station to correctly set up the equipment.

Moon Phases I

Make a clay ball and put it on the end of the pencil. Place the flashlight on a table and turn it on. Hold the ball halfway between you and the light. Observe how much of the part of the ball you can see is lighted. Name the phase of the Moon you modeled.

Station 2

Use the card at the station to correctly set up the equipment.

Moon Phases II

Make a clay ball and put it on the end of the pencil. Place the flashlight on a table and turn it on. Hold the ball out with your right arm into the path of the light. Turn your head. Observe how much of the ball you can see is lighted. Name the phase of the Moon you modeled.

Station 3

Use the card at the station to correctly set up the equipment.

Eclipse

Shape the clay into a model of the Moon and place it on the pencil. Shape a model of Earth using a larger piece of clay. Set the flashlight on one side of a table and set the model of the Moon on the other side of the table. Hold the model of Earth midway between the Moon model and the flashlight. Observe how Earth affects the appearance of the Moon.

Draw a picture of the appearance of the Moon in your model and name the type of eclipse you modeled.

Data Analysis

How do the positions of the Sun, Moon, and Earth affect the appearance of the Moon?

_____

_____

_____

_____

_____

Teacher Instructions and Answers

Teacher Instructions and Answers

**Read each question and choose the best answer.
Then fill in the circle next to the correct answer.**

❶ Choose the word that belongs in the sentence.
_____ have long narrow leaves and do not have woody stems.
- Ⓐ Trees
- ● Grasses
- Ⓒ Flowers
- Ⓓ Evergreens

❷ What kind of tree grows cones to make seeds?
- Ⓕ spring
- Ⓖ summer
- Ⓗ deciduous
- ● coniferous

❸ Choose the word that belongs in the sentence.
Tubes that carry water and minerals from the roots to other parts of the plant are in the _____.
- Ⓐ leaf
- ● stem
- Ⓒ thorn
- Ⓓ flower

❹ What structures help keep a cactus from losing too much water?
- Ⓕ tubers
- Ⓖ thorns
- Ⓗ woody stems
- ● stems with a thick, waxy covering

---

❺ Which seed part stores food for the seed?
- Ⓐ the fruit
- Ⓑ the flower
- ● the seed leaf
- Ⓓ the seed coat

❻ In the forest, Jan picked burs off her pants and dropped them. What did she do by dropping burs?
- Ⓕ She pollinated a plant.
- Ⓖ She did nothing important.
- Ⓗ She left food for the forest animals.
- ● She helped to scatter a plant's seeds.

❼ Look at the illustration below.

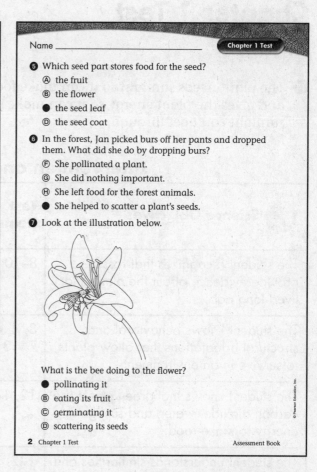

What is the bee doing to the flower?
- ● pollinating it
- Ⓑ eating its fruit
- Ⓒ germinating it
- Ⓓ scattering its seeds

---

❽ Many plants that lived long ago are extinct. How do scientists know about these plants?
- Ⓕ They grow plant fossils.
- ● They found plant fossils.
- Ⓗ They grow plants like them in space.
- Ⓘ They found living plants that are like them.

❾ Look at the object shown in the illustration below.

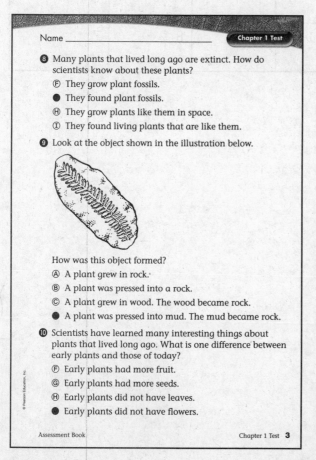

How was this object formed?
- Ⓐ A plant grew in rock.
- Ⓑ A plant was pressed into a rock.
- Ⓒ A plant grew in wood. The wood became rock.
- ● A plant was pressed into mud. The mud became rock.

❿ Scientists have learned many interesting things about plants that lived long ago. What is one difference between early plants and those of today?
- Ⓕ Early plants had more fruit.
- Ⓖ Early plants had more seeds.
- Ⓗ Early plants did not have leaves.
- ● Early plants did not have flowers.

⓫ When a seed starts to grow into a new plant, what is it doing?
- Ⓐ pollinating
- ● germinating
- Ⓒ growing leaves
- Ⓓ creating seedlings

Write the answers to the questions on the lines.

⓬ How do plants get food? (2 points)
The leaves of the plant use sunlight, carbon dioxide, and water to make food.

⓭ How do plants get water? (2 points)
The roots get water from the soil.

Write the answer to the question on a separate sheet of paper.

⓮ Jacob knows that the different parts of a plant help the plant to live and grow. He decides to put two of the same type of plant in his garden. Both plants get the same amount of water. Jacob covers one plant with a cardboard box. Soon the covered plant appears weak and unhealthy.

Explain why covering the plant with the box prevents it from growing.
(4 points)
See page 128 for answer.

Chapter 1 Test

Answer

⑭ The plant needs sunlight so it can make food. The sunlight comes into the leaves and gives the plant energy so it can make sugar. If the box is covering the leaves, the sunlight can't get through.

Intervention and Remediation

★ Science Objectives	Test Items	Student Edition Pages	Quick Study Pages	Workbook Pages
The student recognizes that fossils provide evidence about the plants that lived long ago.	8–10	22–25	10–11	8
The student knows behavioral and structural adaptations that allow plants to survive in an environment.	3, 4, 6, 7, 13	10–19	4–5	5
The student knows that green plants use carbon dioxide, water, and sunlight energy to make food.	12, 14	8–9	2–3	4
The student understands similarities and differences among plants.	1, 2	14–17	6–7	6
The student describes the life cycle of plants.	5, 11	20–21	8–9	7

**Read each question and choose the best answer.
Then fill in the circle next to the correct answer.**

1 What do sea jellies, earthworms, and spiders have in common?
- Ⓐ They all have eight legs.
- Ⓑ They all have stinging body parts.
- Ⓒ They are all animals with backbones.
- ● They are all animals without backbones.

2 A pelican's bill has a pouch that hangs from it. How does this adaptation help it survive?
- ● It helps the bird catch fish.
- Ⓖ It helps the bird store water.
- Ⓗ It helps the bird attack other animals.
- Ⓘ It helps the bird balance itself when it walks.

3 Complete the sentence.
Body parts, such as webbed feet, are inherited, or
- Ⓐ learned.
- Ⓑ never changed.
- ● passed on from parents to offspring.
- Ⓓ not adapted to different environments.

4 Complete the sentence.
An instinct is a behavior that animals
- Ⓕ copy.
- ● are born to do.
- Ⓗ teach each other.
- Ⓘ must learn so they can survive.

5 Which sentence is true?
- Ⓐ Chimpanzees cannot learn from other chimpanzees.
- Ⓑ Chimpanzees have trouble adapting to new environments.
- Ⓒ Chimpanzees are born already knowing how to use sticks to capture insects to eat.
- ● Chimpanzees watch other chimpanzees to learn how to use sticks to capture insects to eat.

6 Look at the illustration below. Think about the life cycle of a monarch butterfly.

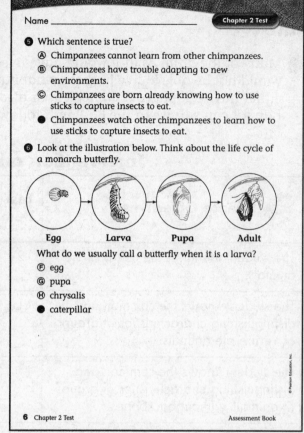

Egg   Larva   Pupa   Adult

What do we usually call a butterfly when it is a larva?
- Ⓕ egg
- Ⓖ pupa
- Ⓗ chrysalis
- ● caterpillar

7 Which kind of animal usually develops inside its mother?
- Ⓐ bird
- Ⓑ insect
- ● mammal
- Ⓓ amphibian

8 Chris finds something that looks like a rock. It is hard and yellow. A dead insect is inside it. What did Chris most likely find?
- Ⓕ a trilobite
- Ⓖ a fossil cast
- Ⓗ a fossil mold
- ● a piece of amber

9 Look at the illustration below of a *T. rex*. Think about the traits of this dinosaur and the traits of living animals.

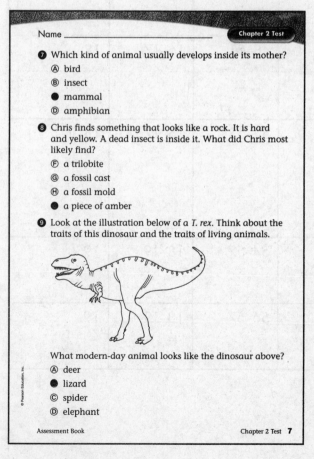

What modern-day animal looks like the dinosaur above?
- Ⓐ deer
- ● lizard
- Ⓒ spider
- Ⓓ elephant

10 A walking stick looks like a real twig. What type of adaptation does a walking stick use for protection?
- Ⓕ armor
- Ⓖ poison
- Ⓗ mimicry
- ● camouflage

Write the answers to the questions on the lines.

11 Amphibians spend part of their lives in water and part on land. Name two members of this group. (2 points)

Answers may vary, but are likely to include two of the

following: frogs, toads, or salamanders.

12 What are the four things all animals need to live? (2 points)

water, oxygen, food, and shelter

Write the answer to the question on a separate sheet of paper.

13 Long ago, the Badlands of South Dakota were hot and wet. Today the Badlands are dry.

Explain how this change in habitat might harm animals. (4 points)
See page 130 for answer.

Chapter 2 Test

Answer

⓭ Many of the animals that would have lived in the hot and wet Badlands long ago would not be able to live in the dry habitat that it has become. The animals would either have adapted over time, left, or died out. Only animals that can survive in a dry habitat can survive in the Badlands today.

Intervention and Remediation

★ Science Objectives	Test Items	Student Edition Pages	Quick Study Pages	Workbook Pages
The student identifies the needs of animals.	12	38–39	12–13	16
The student knows the common and distinguishing characteristics of groups of vertebrate animals.	11	40–41	12–13	16
The student knows the common and distinguishing characteristics of groups of animals without backbones.	1	42–43	12–13	16
The student recognizes that animals go through predictable stages within their life cycles.	6, 7	44–45	14–15	17
The student knows behavioral and structural adaptations that allow plants and animals to survive in an environment.	2, 3, 10	48–51	16–17	18
The student knows that many characteristics of an organism are inherited from the parents of the organism, but that other characteristics are learned from an individual's interactions with the environment.	4, 5	52–53	16–17	18
The student recognizes that fossils provide evidence about animals that lived long ago.	8, 9	54–57	18–19	19
The student understands that changes in the habitat of an organism may be beneficial or harmful.	13	56–57	18–19	19

© Pearson Education, Inc.

Name _____

**Read each question and choose the best answer.
Then fill in the circle next to the correct answer.**

❶ Plants get energy to make food from which of the
following?
- Ⓐ water
- Ⓑ climate
- ● sunlight
- Ⓓ nutrients

❷ Which word best completes the sentence?
Sunlight, water, soil, and climate are the _____ parts of
an ecosystem.
- Ⓕ living
- Ⓖ growing
- ● nonliving
- Ⓘ interacting

❸ Read the paragraph below about a chaparral community.
Then answer the question.

Each part of a chaparral community affects the other parts.
With a lot of rain, more plants grow in the chaparral.
Many animals eat these plants. With much food, the
number of animals increases. In dry years, fewer plants
grow. With less food, the number of animals decreases.

What happens to the number of animals in years when
there is little rain?
- Ⓐ The number increases.
- ● The number decreases.
- Ⓒ The number does not change.
- Ⓓ The number decreases and then it increases.

Assessment Book   Chapter 3 Test **9**

Name _____

❹ Grasshoppers and bison live in which type of ecosystem?
- Ⓕ desert
- Ⓖ tundra
- ● grasslands
- Ⓘ tropical forest

❺ What is the biggest difference between a desert and a
tropical forest?
- Ⓐ how cold each gets
- Ⓑ how warm each gets
- Ⓒ how much life each has
- ● how much rain each gets

❻ In which ecosystem would you find wolves, caribou, brown
bears, and eagles?
- Ⓕ desert
- Ⓖ prairie
- ● tundra
- Ⓘ tropical forest

❼ Oak, maple, and beech trees drop their leaves in the fall.
In which ecosystem are they found?
- Ⓐ tundra
- Ⓑ tropical forest
- ● deciduous forest
- Ⓓ coniferous forest

10 Chapter 3 Test   Assessment Book

Name _____

❽ Choose the best word to complete the sentence.
Lakes, ponds, rivers, and streams are examples of _____
ecosystems.
- Ⓕ dry
- Ⓖ wetland
- Ⓗ saltwater
- ● freshwater

❾ Read the chart. Use what you learn to answer the question.

Water Ecosystems	
Type of Water	**Examples of Plants and Animals**
Saltwater	Corals, sea dragons, cuttlefish, clams, crabs, algae, otters, seals, shrimp, whales, starfish
Freshwater	Manatees, bass, cormorants, alligators, red mangrove trees, grasses, bears
Where Freshwater and Saltwater Meet	Fish, crabs

In which type of water would a whale live?
- ● saltwater
- Ⓑ freshwater
- Ⓒ in any kind of water ecosystem
- Ⓓ where freshwater and saltwater meet

Assessment Book   Chapter 3 Test **11**

Name _____

Write the answers to the questions on the lines.

❿ Why does a tundra have few trees? (2 points)
Tree roots cannot grow into the frozen soil in a tundra.

⓫ What are two ways plants in an animal's habitat help
meet its needs? (2 points)
Possible answers: animal eats the plants; animals can use the

plants for shelter.

**Write the answer to the question on a separate sheet of
paper.**

⓬ Look at the illustration below.

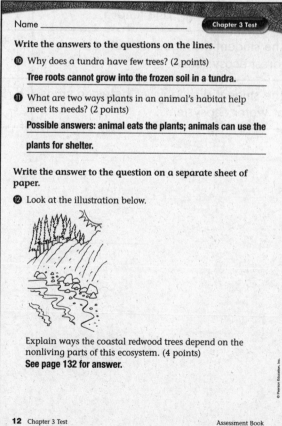

Explain ways the coastal redwood trees depend on the
nonliving parts of this ecosystem. (4 points)
See page 132 for answer.

12 Chapter 3 Test   Assessment Book

Assessment Book   Answer Key **131**

Chapter 3 Test

Answer

12 The coastal redwood trees use sunlight to make their own food. They also need soil, air, and water to survive.

Intervention and Remediation

⭐ Science Objectives	Test Items	Student Edition Pages	Quick Study Pages	Workbook Pages
The student knows that some source of energy is needed for organisms to stay alive and grow.	1	70–71	20–21	26
The student understands various ways that animals depend on plants for survival (for example, food, shelter, oxygen).	2, 11, 12	72–73	20–21	26
The student knows that the size of a population is dependent upon the available resources within its community.	3	74–75	20–21	26
The student distinguishes between grassland, desert, and tundra.	4–6, 10	76–81	22–23	27
The student distinguishes between forest ecosystems.	5, 7	82–85	24–25	28
The student distinguishes between kinds of water ecosystems.	8, 9	86–89	26–27	29

Assessment Book

Read each question and choose the best answer.
Then fill in the circle next to the correct answer.

1 What is the main reason prairie dogs live together?
- ● for protection
- Ⓑ to move faster
- Ⓒ for appearance
- Ⓓ to raise their young together

2 Which word **best** completes the sentence?
The population of lemmings changes when the amount of _____ in their environment changes.
- Ⓕ habitats
- ● resources
- Ⓗ food chains
- Ⓘ competition

3 Which word **best** completes the sentence?
A _____ is a living thing that breaks down waste and things that have died.
- Ⓐ predator
- Ⓑ producer
- Ⓒ consumer
- ● decomposer

4 Small trees trying to get the same resources as taller trees is an example of which of the following?
- Ⓕ producers
- Ⓖ consumers
- Ⓗ interaction
- ● competition

5 Look at the chart below. Think about how each living thing gets the energy it needs to live.

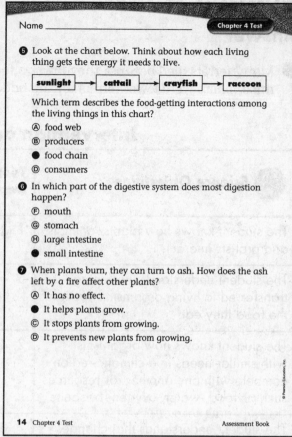

sunlight → cattail → crayfish → raccoon

Which term describes the food-getting interactions among the living things in this chart?
- Ⓐ food web
- Ⓑ producers
- ● food chain
- Ⓓ consumers

6 In which part of the digestive system does most digestion happen?
- Ⓕ mouth
- Ⓖ stomach
- Ⓗ large intestine
- ● small intestine

7 When plants burn, they can turn to ash. How does the ash left by a fire affect other plants?
- Ⓐ It has no effect.
- ● It helps plants grow.
- Ⓒ It stops plants from growing.
- Ⓓ It prevents new plants from growing.

8 Look at the illustration below. It shows a place that was once dry.

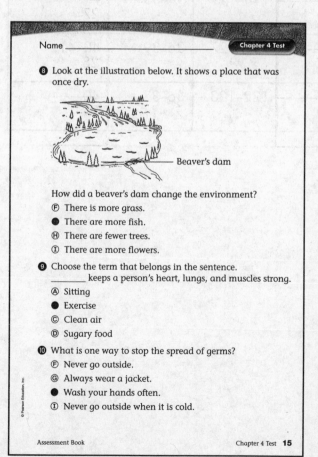

Beaver's dam

How did a beaver's dam change the environment?
- Ⓕ There is more grass.
- ● There are more fish.
- Ⓗ There are fewer trees.
- Ⓘ There are more flowers.

9 Choose the term that belongs in the sentence.
_____ keeps a person's heart, lungs, and muscles strong.
- Ⓐ Sitting
- ● Exercise
- Ⓒ Clean air
- Ⓓ Sugary food

10 What is one way to stop the spread of germs?
- Ⓕ Never go outside.
- Ⓖ Always wear a jacket.
- ● Wash your hands often.
- Ⓘ Never go outside when it is cold.

Write the answers to the questions on the lines.

11 People obtain the things they need to live from the environment. What do people need to survive? (2 points)

food, water, shelter, air, and a clean environment

12 Look at the illustration. Explain how yucca moths and yucca plants help each other. (2 points)

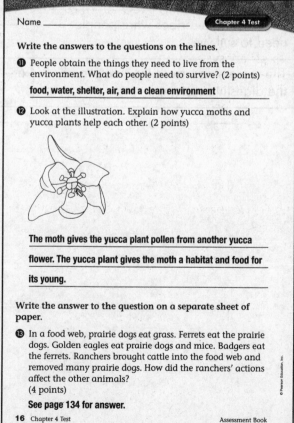

The moth gives the yucca plant pollen from another yucca

flower. The yucca plant gives the moth a habitat and food for

its young.

Write the answer to the question on a separate sheet of paper.

13 In a food web, prairie dogs eat grass. Ferrets eat the prairie dogs. Golden eagles eat prairie dogs and mice. Badgers eat the ferrets. Ranchers brought cattle into the food web and removed many prairie dogs. How did the ranchers' actions affect the other animals?
(4 points)

See page 134 for answer.

Chapter 4 Test

Answer

⑬ Many ferrets died because they had no food to eat. The golden eagles had to eat more mice. There were fewer ferrets for the badgers to eat. They had to find other food.

Intervention and Remediation

⭐ Science Objectives	Test Items	Student Edition Pages	Quick Study Pages	Workbook Pages
The student knows how plants, animals, and protists interact.	1, 3, 12	104–105, 118–119	28–29, 34–35	36, 39
The student understands that energy is transferred to living organisms through the food they eat.	5	106–107	30–31	37
The student knows how organisms with similar needs in a climatic region compete with one another for resources such as food, water, oxygen, or space.	2, 4	110–113, 118–119	32–35	38–39
The student understands that changes in the habitat of an organism may be beneficial or harmful.	7, 8, 13	108–109, 114–119	30–31, 34–35	37, 39
The student describes what people need to survive.	9–11	120–127	36–39	40–41
The student describes the function of the digestive system.	6	122–123	36–37	40

© Pearson Education, Inc.

Read each question and choose the best answer.
Then fill in the circle next to the correct answer.

1 Plants need leaves to
Ⓐ shade the plant from the Sun.
● make sugar as food for the plant.
Ⓒ take in water for the plant to live.
Ⓓ make carbon dioxide for us to breathe.

2 What plant part takes water and minerals from the soil, holds the plant in its place, and stores food?
Ⓕ seeds
Ⓖ leaves
● root system
Ⓘ stem system

3 Look at the illustration below.

What kind of tree does the picture show?
Ⓐ grassy
Ⓑ coniferous
Ⓒ evergreen
● deciduous

---

4 A pika is a vertebrate animal that has hair, breathes air through its lungs, and feeds milk to its young. What animal group does a pika belong to?
Ⓕ fish
Ⓖ birds
Ⓗ reptiles
● mammals

5 A bear does not have to learn how to hibernate. Knowing how to hibernate is
● an instinct.
Ⓑ an adaptation.
Ⓒ a practiced skill.
Ⓓ a previously learned trait.

6 How does a mammal usually develop?
Ⓕ as a larva
Ⓖ as a tadpole
● inside its mother
Ⓘ inside a chrysalis

7 If a habitat does not have the right kind of food for a certain kind of animal, what is most likely to happen?
Ⓐ The animal will change its diet.
Ⓑ The animal will bring its own food.
● The animal will move to a new habitat.
Ⓓ The animal will have its young there but not live there.

---

8 Grasshoppers eat grass. Which ecosystem is best for grasshoppers?
Ⓕ forest
Ⓖ desert
Ⓗ tundra
● grassland

9 A bass lives among the weeds of lakes and streams. Which water ecosystem is best for a bass?
Ⓐ pond
Ⓑ saltwater
● freshwater
Ⓓ where freshwater and saltwater mix

10 Look at the illustration below.

How do prairie dogs interact with their group?
Ⓕ They hunt for food together.
Ⓖ They run away from the group.
Ⓗ They prefer to live away from the group.
● They stand watch and warn the group of danger.

---

11 Living things that eat plants and animals are called
Ⓐ producers.
Ⓑ carnivores.
● omnivores.
Ⓓ herbivores.

Write the answers to the questions on the lines.

12 List the following plants and animals in the order that they would be in a food chain: ferret, prairie dog, bobcat, grass (2 points)

grass, prairie dog, ferret, bobcat

13 A tree in a forest fell to the ground and started decaying. Why is it a good idea to leave the tree there and not remove it? (2 points)

The decaying log gives seedlings a place to grow into new

trees. The log also holds water better than the soil.

Write your answers to the question on a separate sheet of paper.

14 Several of your classmates have the flu. Some stay home. Some come to school.

Explain which is the better thing to do and why. Also name something you can do to stop the spread of germs. (4 points)
See page 134 for answer.

Unit A Test

Answer

14 It is better for the classmates with the flu to stay home. The classmates who do not come to school will not spread the flu to others. The germs of those who come to school might cause others to become ill, too. Washing your hands often can help stop the spread of germs.

Unit A Test Talk Answers

Strategy 1   page 22

1. I need to find out what Paul Sereno decided to become while he was in college.
2. I need to find out what Paul Sereno did with his brothers when he was young.
3. I need to find out what a paleontologist is.

Strategy 2   page 23

1. I found the answer in paragraph 1, sentence 4.
2. I found the answer in paragraph 1, sentence 1.
3. I found the answer in paragraph 1, sentence 4, and paragraph 2, sentence 1.

Strategy 3   page 24

1. C a paleontologist
2. F went on nature hikes
3. D a scientist who studies ancient life

Strategy 4   page 25

1. **My Notes:** a paleontologist, a scientist who studies ancient life
   My Answer: While in college, Paul Sereno decided to become a paleontologist. He wanted to be a scientist who studies ancient life.
2. **My Notes:** study ancient life, try to find fossils, piece together the story of what life was like long ago
   My Answer: Paleontologists study ancient life by looking at fossils. The scientists try to piece together the story of life long ago.

Strategy 5   page 26

1. To find the answer, I will look at the picture to see what *Suchomimus* looked like.
   My Answer: *Suchomimus* looked like a big dinosaur with a long skull and the teeth of a crocodile.
2. To find the answer, I will look at the picture and see where the fossils are found.
   My Answer: Fossils can sometimes be found in the desert.

Strategy 6   page 27

1. To score higher, Carla needs to change "crocodile" to "dinosaur" because "crocodile" is wrong. She also needs to take out "When he was young, Paul Sereno collected insects" because that is not important.
2. To score higher, Derek needs to take out "Paleontologists have to study hard when they are in college" because that isn't important. He also needs to take out "A giant tooth is a clue" because that is wrong.

Unit A Writing Prompt

Choose an ecosystem. Write a story that tells about the plants and animals that live there. Include details about how the plants and animals interact.

Grade 3 Writing Scoring Guide [Use with Unit A]

Score	Focus	Organization	Support	Conventions	Science Content
6	well focused on the topic	logical organizational pattern with a beginning, middle, and conclusion; excellent use of transitional devices	ample development of the supporting ideas, demonstrates a sense of completeness or wholeness; precision in word choice	generally correct subject/verb agreement and verb and noun forms; complete sentences except when fragments are used purposefully; a variety of sentence structures	no errors
5	focused on the topic	organizational pattern, with a few lapses; good use of transitional devices	adequate development of the supporting ideas with a sense of completeness or wholeness; adequate word choice but may lack precision	occasional errors in subject/verb agreement and in standard forms of verbs and nouns, but not enough to impede communication; generally follows conventions of punctuation, capitalization, and spelling; most sentences complete; some variety of sentence structures	few errors
4	fairly well focused on the topic but some loosely related information	evidence of an organizational pattern and transitional devices, but with some lapses	supporting ideas sometimes contain specifics and details but sometimes not developed; generally adequate word choice	demonstrates knowledge of conventions of punctuation and capitalization; correct spelling of commonly used words; an attempt to use a variety of sentence structures, although some are simple	some minor errors
3	generally focused on the topic but some extraneous information	organizational pattern attempted with some transitional devices, but some lapses	some supporting ideas not developed with specifics and details; adequate but limited word choice, occasionally vague	demonstrates knowledge of conventions of punctuation and capitalization, but some errors; correct spelling of commonly used words; an attempt to use a variety of sentence structures, although most are simple	1 or 2 significant errors
2	slightly related to topic	little evidence of an organizational pattern or transitional devices	development of supporting ideas often inadequate or illogical; limited or immature word choice	frequent errors in basic punctuation and capitalization; commonly used words frequently misspelled; primarily simple sentence constructions	significant errors
1	minimally addresses the topic	does not exhibit an organizational pattern	little, if any, development of supporting ideas, and usually provided through lists, clichés, and limited or immature word choice	frequent errors in spelling, capitalization, punctuation, and sentence structure; sentences primarily simple constructions	gross errors

Unscorable: The response has one or more of these problems: the response is not related to what the prompt requested the student to do; the response is simply a rewording of the prompt; the response is a copy of a published work; the student refused to write; the response is written in a foreign language; the response is illegible; the response is incomprehensible (words are arranged in such a way that no meaning is conveyed)

Anchor Paper: 6 points

Choose an ecosystem. Write a story that tells about the plants and animals that live there. Include details about how the plants and animals interact.

The coyote ran with the pack in the early morning hours of the day. She needed food for her pups. She hoped to find a ground squirrel. Suddenly she saw a head pop out of a burrow near some rocks. Quietly, she moved closer. But the squirrel was too fast. It ran back into its burrow.

She didn't see another squirrel. There weren't many this year. It was a dry year. So there wasn't much food. There weren't enough nuts and other food for the little animals to eat. So the big animals went hungry too.

Later that morning, the coyote warmed herself in the sunlight. She watched her pups play among the chaparral. She had only two pups this year. Living in dry California wasn't easy. Perhaps she would be luckier in the hunt that evening.

Score Point: 6

The writing focuses well on the topic. The organization has a beginning, middle, and conclusion with excellent use of transitional devices. The writing exhibits ample development of supporting ideas, demonstrates a sense of completeness or wholeness and a precision in word choice. Grammar usage is generally correct with subject/verb agreement and proper verb and noun forms. The paper is written in complete sentences except when fragments are used purposefully and there is variety in sentence structures. There are no errors in content.

Anchor Paper: 5 points

Choose an ecosystem. Write a story that tells about the plants and animals that live there. Include details about how the plants and animals interact.

> The cool night air felt good after the long hot day. A snake slithered across the sand. Was it looking for dinner or a place to rest for the night? A small bird ate fruit from a yucca plant. A lizard came out of its hiding place to look for food.
>
> "I love the desert," said a bobcat. She started to stir from her resting place on a rock. It was time to hunt. "Will I catch a bird or a small animal tonight?" she wondered.

Score Point: 5

The writing is focused on the topic. The paper is organized with only a few lapses and has good transitional devices. The writing is adequately developed, uses supporting ideas with a sense of completeness or wholeness. The word choice is adequate but may lack precision. There are occasional errors in subject/verb agreement and in standard forms of verbs and nouns, but not enough to impede communication. The conventions of punctuation, capitalization, and spelling are generally followed. Most sentences are complete and there is some variety of sentence structures. There are a few errors in content.

Anchor Paper: 4 points

Choose an ecosystem. Write a story that tells about the plants and animals that live there. Include details about how the plants and animals interact.

Altsoba watches as a pack of wolves runs across the tundra. He points to an eagle flying overhead. "Little Brother, look at the eagle and the wolves. They are hunters here. Just like us."

"I want to see a bear," says Little Brother. "I don't," the older brother answers.

Little Brother picks at the hard ground. Even though it is summer, the soil is still frozen. Little Brother sees a caribou. He watches it eat the liken. "Why do the caribou eat liken? Yuck."

"It is the only plant that grows in the frozen soil," says Altoba. "Let's find something to eat."

Score Point: 4

The writing focuses fairly well on the topic but contains some loosely related information. The paper shows evidence of an organizational pattern and transitional devices but has some lapses. The supporting ideas, while sometimes containing specifics and details, are sometimes also not developed. The word choice is generally adequate. The writing demonstrates knowledge of conventions of punctuation and capitalization and correct spelling of commonly used words. There is an attempt to use a variety of sentence structures, although some are simple. There are some minor errors in content.

Anchor Paper: 3 points

Choose an ecosystem. Write a story that tells about the plants and animals that live there. Include details about how the plants and animals interact.

Beaver moved slowly as it pulled the log through the forest. He pulled it to the side of the stream. He had been working all day. But the dam was not done. He stopped to eat a snack of beetles that he had dug up from a tree trunk. He listened to nearby woodpeckers, tapping on trees. I must get back to work he thought. Trees dropped their leaves. Frogs croaked.

Score Point: 3

The writing generally focuses on the topic but has some extraneous information. The paper shows an organizational pattern with some attempts to use transitional devices but some lapses occur. There are some supporting ideas but they are not developed with specifics and details. Word choice is adequate but limited and occasionally vague. The writing demonstrates knowledge of conventions of punctuation and capitalization but has some errors. Commonly used words are correctly spelled. An attempt is made to use a variety of sentence structures, although most are simple. There are one or two significant errors in content.

Anchor Paper: 2 points

Choose an ecosystem. Write a story that tells about the plants and animals that live there. Include details about how the plants and animals interact.

> A black bear ate berrys near a pond. "Watch out," it grumbled at a moose nearby. Go find another place to eat your water lilies. The moose found another place to eat. It was a cold winter day. Too cold to argue with a bear.

Score Point: 2

The writing is slightly related to the topic. There is little evidence of an organizational pattern or use of transitional devices. The development of supporting ideas is often inadequate or illogical. Word choice is limited or immature. The paper has frequent errors in basic punctuation and capitalization. Commonly used words are frequently misspelled. Sentence constructions are primarily simple. There are significant errors in content.

Grade 3

Anchor Paper: 1 point

Choose an ecosystem. Write a story that tells about the plants and animals that live there. Include details about how the plants and animals interact.

> Billy Bison chewed the prairy grass. His sister Babe got a drink from the creek. A grasshopper jumped from a wildflower. Billy loved the grass. It was wet and crunchy. He walked to the forest edge. He wanted to take a nap.

Score Point: 1

The writing minimally addresses the topic and does not exhibit an organizational pattern. There are little, if any, supporting ideas and those ideas are usually provided through lists, clichés, and limited or immature word choice. The writing shows frequent errors in spelling, capitalization, punctuation, and sentence structure. Sentences are primarily simple constructions. There are gross errors in content.

© Pearson Education, Inc.

Unit A Performance Test Instructions
Collecting Data on Bottled Water

Description: Students are asked to compare the clarity and smell of two water samples, to filter clay particles out of them, and to test the acidity of each sample.

Purpose: To evaluate a student's ability to collect data and record observations about two water samples and to make a recommendation as to which one would be acceptable drinking water.

Science Process Skill: Collecting Data

Time: Stations 1, 2, and 3 are designed to take students 40–45 minutes to complete.

Teacher Instructions

Station 1
Materials
> clay soil
> vinegar
> water
> 2 plastic 2-liter bottles labeled "A" and "B"
> 2 plastic cups labeled "A" and "B" for each student
> hand lens
> grease pencil
> paper towels
> Blackline Masters: pages 29 and 147

Preparation
1. Make copies of the blackline masters. Page 147 provides station setup instructions. Students can use page 29 to record their answers.
2. Prepare water sample A by adding 50 cc of clay soil and 30 mL of vinegar to 2 liters of water in bottle A. Shake sample well.
3. Prepare water sample B by adding 50 cc of clay soil to 2 liters of water in bottle B. Shake sample well.
4. Mark each of the plastic cups with a fill line. Each sample should be about 120 mL.
5. Have paper towels on hand in case of spills.

Suggestions for teachers
- Use very fine clay for this activity so that clay will remain in suspension after it is mixed with water. Water samples should look cloudy.
- Students will be able to see particles of clay in the water.
- Remind students to take their two water samples to Station 2.

Station 2

Materials

2 sheets of filter paper for each student
2 water samples labeled "A" and "B" from Station 1
2 plastic cups labeled "A" and "B" for each student
2 plastic funnels labeled "A" and "B"
hand lens
paper towels
trash container for used filter paper
grease pencil
Blackline Masters: pages 29 and 147

Preparation

1. Make copies of the blackline masters. Use page 147 to provide station setup instructions. Students can use page 29 to record their answers.
2. Students will use their water samples from Station 1.
3. Line each funnel with filter paper.
4. Have paper towels on hand in case of spills.

Suggestions for teachers

- Students will find that most of the clay in the water will be trapped by the filter paper.

Station 3

Materials

blue litmus paper
2 water samples labeled "A" and "B" from Station 2
150 mL sample of drinking or tap water labeled "standard"
plastic cup
paper towels
trash container for used litmus paper
Blackline Masters: pages 30 and 148

Preparation

1. Make copies of the blackline masters. Page 148 provides station setup instructions. Students can use page 30 to record their answers.
2. Dip a blue litmus strip into the standard sample. Leave strip next to standard sample for students to examine.
3. Demonstrate for students how to use litmus test strips properly.
4. Have paper towels on hand in case of spills.

Suggestions for teachers

- Students should be able to notice the vinegar smell in sample A.
- Blue litmus paper will turn pink or red when treated with an acid. It remains blue if the sample is neutral or basic. Sample A should test as acidic.

Station 1

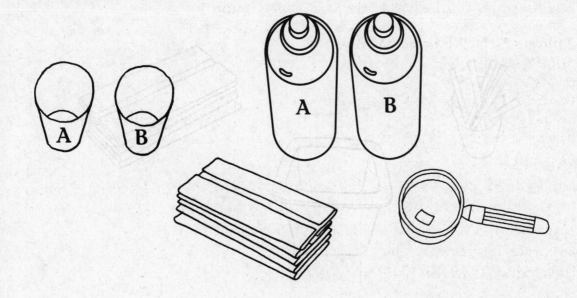

Be sure that the materials are set up like this before you leave this station.

Station 2

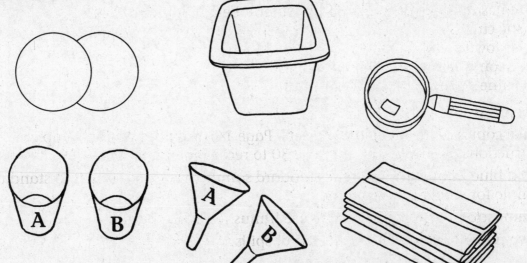

Be sure that the materials are set up like this before you leave this station.

Station 3

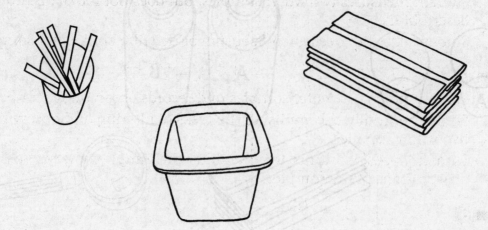

Be sure that the materials are set up like this before you leave this station.

Scoring Guide

Station 1

3 points Student accurately measures and describes two water samples.

2 points Student measures two water samples, but does not make accurate descriptions.

1 point Student does not accurately measure or describe both water samples.

Station 2

3 points Student filters two water samples and records observations for both.

2 points Student partially accomplishes the tasks of filtering and observing the two water samples.

1 point Student needs assistance to either filter the samples or describe the observations of the samples.

Station 3

3 points Student tests each sample and accurately compares results with the standard sample.

2 points Student tests each sample but does not accurately compare results with the standard sample.

1 point Student does not record results of sample testing.

Data Analysis

3 points Student recommends a type of water based on all three tests.

2 points Student recommends a type of water based on some but not all of the tests.

1 point Student needs assistance in making a recommendation and/or does not consider data from any of the tests.

Total Score

Points	Percent equivalent
12	100
11	92
10	83
9	75
8	67
7	58
6	50
5	42
4	33
3	25
2	16
1	8

Collecting Data on Bottled Water

Decide if two different water sources should be used for bottled water.

Station 1

Use the card at the station to correctly set up the equipment.

Water Sample Observation

Pour water from bottle A into cup A up to the fill line. Do the same with bottle B and cup B.

Observe how the water in each sample looks and smells.

Record your observations of water samples A and B.

Sample A: **very cloudy with particles**

Sample B: **cloudy with small particles**

Station 2

Use the card at the station to correctly set up the equipment.

Water Test 1

Pour sample A through funnel A into cup A. Do the same with sample B, funnel B, and cup B.

Observe each filter and each sample of filtered water.

Record your observations of water samples A and B.

Sample A: **looks clearer than before but still cloudy**

Sample B: **looks a lot clearer than before**

Station 3

Use the card at the station to correctly set up the equipment.

Water Test 2

Use the litmus paper to test each sample. Compare the color of your litmus strips with the color of the litmus strip labeled "standard."

Record your observations in the data table.

Water sample	Clearness	Odor	Reacts with litmus paper
Standard	clear water	no odor	Blue, sample is neutral or basic
Sample A	fairly clear	vinegar smell	Pink/red, sample is acidic
Sample B	fairly clear	no odor	Blue, sample is neutral or basic

Data Analysis

Now you have completed the water tests. Use your data and what you know about water to answer the following question.

Would either of the two sources provide water that would be good drinking water? Explain.

Students should not recommend sample A based on its

continued cloudiness, odor, and acidic litmus test. Students could

recommend sample B, but would need to note that the water

needs to be filtered to be good to use.

Name _____

**Read each question and choose the best answer.
Then fill in the circle next to the correct answer.**

❶ What makes up two-thirds of your body?
Ⓐ skin
● water
Ⓒ oxygen
Ⓓ muscles

❷ Choose the term that belongs in the sentence.
People use the power of moving water to make _____.
● electricity
Ⓖ generators
Ⓗ wind power
Ⓘ solar power

❸ About how much of Earth's surface is covered with water?
Ⓐ 10%
Ⓑ 25%
Ⓒ 67%
● 75%

❹ What is water that seeps down and collects in underground spaces called?
Ⓕ saltwater
Ⓖ well water
Ⓗ water vapor
● groundwater

Name _____

❺ Why are wetlands an important environmental resource?
Ⓐ They help to flood dry areas.
● They are homes for many animals.
Ⓒ They decrease the water vapor supply.
Ⓓ They decrease the groundwater supply.

❻ What process occurs when water changes to a gas?
Ⓕ melting
● evaporation
Ⓗ precipitation
Ⓘ condensation

❼ At what temperature does water freeze solid?
● 0°C
Ⓑ 10°C
Ⓒ 32°C
Ⓓ 100°C

❽ During the water cycle, what generally happens to the water after evaporation?
Ⓕ It falls to Earth as precipitation.
● It condenses and forms a cloud.
Ⓗ It evaporates until it is entirely gone.
Ⓘ It seeps into Earth as groundwater.

Name _____

❾ Look at the illustration below.

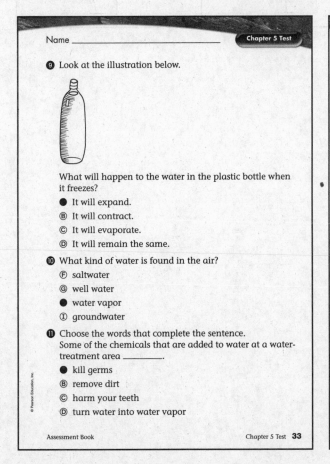

What will happen to the water in the plastic bottle when it freezes?
● It will expand.
Ⓑ It will contract.
Ⓒ It will evaporate.
Ⓓ It will remain the same.

❿ What kind of water is found in the air?
Ⓕ saltwater
Ⓖ well water
● water vapor
Ⓘ groundwater

⓫ Choose the words that complete the sentence.
Some of the chemicals that are added to water at a water-treatment area _____.
● kill germs
Ⓑ remove dirt
Ⓒ harm your teeth
Ⓓ turn water into water vapor

Name _____

Write the answer to the question on the lines.

⓬ Why must water that people use be clean? Give two reasons. (2 points)

Germs in water can make people sick. Dirt or salt in water

can harm machines.

Write the answer to the question on a separate sheet of paper.

⓭ Look at the illustration below.

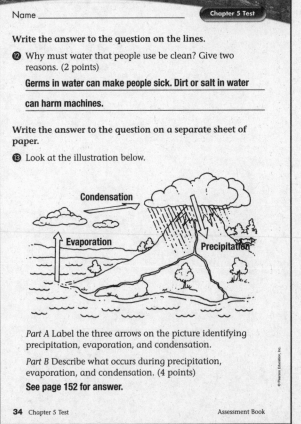

Part A Label the three arrows on the picture identifying precipitation, evaporation, and condensation.

Part B Describe what occurs during precipitation, evaporation, and condensation. (4 points)
See page 152 for answer.

© Pearson Education, Inc.

Chapter 5 Test

Answer

⓭ Check students' pictures. Possible answer: During evaporation, the Sun's energy causes water on Earth to evaporate and become water vapor. During condensation, the water vapor rises into cooler air and forms droplets which cling together and form clouds. When water droplets in clouds become too heavy to float in the air, they fall to Earth as precipitation.

Intervention and Remediation

⭐ Science Objectives	Test Items	Student Edition Pages	Quick Study Pages	Workbook Pages
The student recognizes the importance of water to living things.	1, 2, 5, 11, 12	150–155, 160–161	40–41	48–49
The student knows that approximately 75 percent of the surface of the Earth is covered by water.	3, 4, 10	154–155	40–41	48
The student understands how water changes state.	6, 7, 9	156–157	42–43	49
The student understands the stages of the water cycle.	8, 13	158–159	42–43	49

Assessment Book

Read each question and choose the best answer.
Then fill in the circle next to the correct answer.

❶ On what kind of day would you see white, fluffy clouds?
Ⓐ a cold, snowy day
Ⓑ a cool, stormy day
Ⓒ a warm, rainy day
● a warm, bright day

❷ What type of winter weather will there likely be in a town in eastern Washington?
● The weather will be cold and dry.
Ⓖ The weather will be cool and wet.
Ⓗ The weather will be mild and wet.
Ⓘ The weather will be warm and dry.

❸ Look at the illustration below.

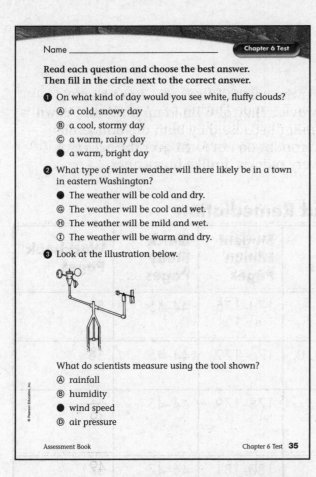

What do scientists measure using the tool shown?
Ⓐ rainfall
Ⓑ humidity
● wind speed
Ⓓ air pressure

❹ A scientist needs to measure the air pressure. What tool should the scientist use?
● barometer
Ⓖ rain gauge
Ⓗ hygrometer
Ⓘ thermometer

❺ What type of severe storm is a spinning column of air that touches the ground?
● tornado
Ⓑ blizzard
Ⓒ hurricane
Ⓓ thunderstorm

❻ Where do hurricanes form?
Ⓕ over deserts
Ⓖ over dry land
Ⓗ over ice sheets
● over warm oceans

❼ When should people with breathing difficulties avoid the outdoors?
Ⓐ when there is acid rain
● when there is a smog alert
Ⓒ when there is heavy snowfall
Ⓓ when there is a thunderstorm watch

❽ What harmful substance do cars and trucks cause in the air?
● ozone
Ⓖ oxygen
Ⓗ nitrogen
Ⓘ carbon dioxide

❾ If the National Weather Service puts out a tornado warning, when is a tornado likely to strike?
Ⓐ in a few days
Ⓑ in a few hours
Ⓒ during the next month
● during the next few minutes

❿ What does a picture of the sun behind a cloud mean on a weather map?
Ⓕ rainy weather
Ⓖ sunny weather
Ⓗ stormy weather
● partly cloudy weather

⓫ What type of storm has low temperatures, strong winds, and heavy snowfall?
Ⓐ cyclone
Ⓑ tornado
● blizzard
Ⓓ hurricane

Write the answers to the question on the lines.

⓬ A scientist is using the instrument shown below. What is the name of the instrument? What is it used for? (2 points)

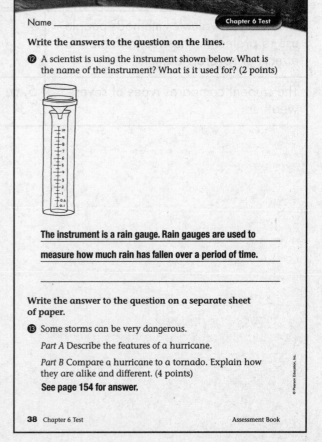

The instrument is a rain gauge. Rain gauges are used to

measure how much rain has fallen over a period of time.

_____

Write the answer to the question on a separate sheet of paper.

⓭ Some storms can be very dangerous.

Part A Describe the features of a hurricane.

Part B Compare a hurricane to a tornado. Explain how they are alike and different. (4 points)
See page 154 for answer.

Chapter 6 Test

Answer

⑬ A hurricane is a huge storm that forms over the ocean. Hurricanes have heavy rainfall, strong winds, and produce huge waves. They also build up and wind down gradually. Hurricanes and tornados are similar because they both are dangerous storms that have strong winds. However, tornados do not form over the ocean or produce huge waves. Tornados also form very quickly, unlike hurricanes.

Intervention and Remediation

⭐ Science Objectives	Test Items	Student Edition Pages	Quick Study Pages	Workbook Pages
The student describes the parts of weather.	1	174–175	44–45	56
The student identifies ways of measuring and predicting weather.	3, 4, 10, 12	176–179	44–45	56
The student identifies and evaluates ways people affect weather through their daily activities.	7, 8	178–179	44–45	56
The student describes ways weather depicts natural patterns of change.	2	180–181	46–47	57
The student evaluates methods people use to protect themselves from the effects of severe weather.	9	182–183	46–47	57
The student compares types of severe weather.	5, 6, 11, 13	182–183	46–47	57

Name _____

Read each question and choose the best answer. Then fill in the circle next to the correct answer.

❶ One way to tell rocks apart is by looking at the size of the bits of minerals that make up each rock. What is this physical property called?

Ⓐ color

Ⓑ luster

● texture

Ⓓ heaviness

❷ How is metamorphic rock formed?

Ⓕ Pressure over time binds sediments into rock.

● Heat and/or pressure change the minerals in a rock.

Ⓗ A hot mixture of gases and minerals cools into rock.

Ⓘ Water slowly wears down minerals, turning them into rock.

❸ Look at the illustration below.

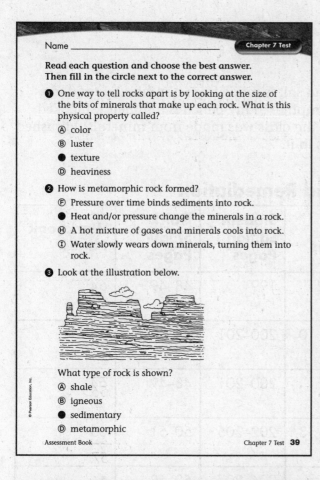

What type of rock is shown?

Ⓐ shale

Ⓑ igneous

● sedimentary

Ⓓ metamorphic

Name _____

❹ Which type of particles found in soil are the smallest?

Ⓕ silt

● clay

Ⓗ sand

Ⓘ shale

❺ What layer of soil includes rock particles mixed with the dark products of decay?

Ⓐ silt

Ⓑ clay

● topsoil

Ⓓ subsoil

❻ What mineral is crushed and ground into salt that is used to season food?

● halite

Ⓖ quartz

Ⓗ fluorite

Ⓘ graphite

❼ Which two properties would be best to use to identify a mineral?

Ⓐ color and luster

Ⓑ shape and luster

Ⓒ size and magnetism

● hardness and streak

Name _____

❽ Where do the nutrients in the soil mainly come from?

Ⓕ rainfall

Ⓖ running water

Ⓗ living plants and animals

● decay of plants and animals

❾ Look at the illustration below.

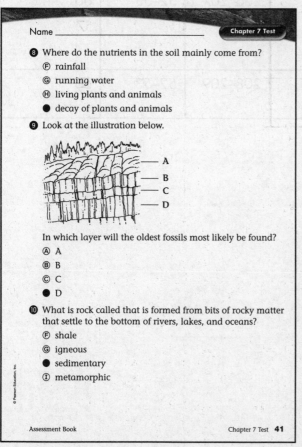

In which layer will the oldest fossils most likely be found?

Ⓐ A

Ⓑ B

Ⓒ C

● D

❿ What is rock called that is formed from bits of rocky matter that settle to the bottom of rivers, lakes, and oceans?

Ⓕ shale

Ⓖ igneous

● sedimentary

Ⓘ metamorphic

Name _____

Write the answers to the questions on the lines.

⓫ Why is the mixture of soil called loam good for growing plants? (2 points)

Loam is made of sand, silt, and clay. It has high amounts of decayed matter and minerals and therefore has many nutrients. Loam soils also hold onto water loosely enough for plant roots to soak it up.

⓬ What physical properties can you use to tell rocks apart? (2 points)

Rocks can be told apart by looking at their physical properties such as color, what minerals they are made of, and the texture (size of the grains).

Write the answer to the question on a separate sheet of paper.

⓭ People use minerals almost every day. Identify four ways that you have used minerals today. (4 points)
See page 156 for answer.

© Pearson Education, Inc.

Chapter 7 Test

Answer

⑬ Possible answer: I used salt on my eggs and salt is made from a mineral; I used my pencil to solve a math problem and the graphite in my pencil is a mineral; I looked out the window to check the weather and the glass was made from minerals; I brushed my teeth and the toothpaste has minerals in it.

Intervention and Remediation

★ Science Objectives	Test Items	Student Edition Pages	Quick Study Pages	Workbook Pages
The student compares different kinds of rocks.	1, 12	199	48–49	64
The student explains how rocks are formed.	2, 3, 10	200–201	48–49	64
The student describes how rocks can help explain life over time.	9	200–201	48–49	64
The student compares different kinds of minerals.	6, 7, 13	202–205	50–51	65
The student knows that some changes in the Earth's surface are due to slow processes and some changes are due to rapid processes.	5, 8	206–207	52–53	66
The student compares properties of different kinds of soil.	4, 11	208–209	52–53	66

Name _____

Read each question and choose the best answer.
Then fill in the circle next to the correct answer.

1 Look at the illustration below.

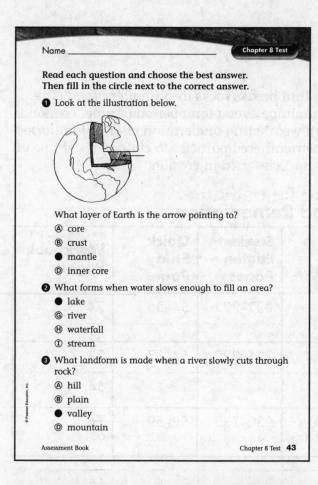

What layer of Earth is the arrow pointing to?

Ⓐ core

Ⓑ crust

● mantle

Ⓓ inner core

2 What forms when water slows enough to fill an area?

● lake

Ⓖ river

Ⓗ waterfall

Ⓘ stream

3 What landform is made when a river slowly cuts through rock?

Ⓐ hill

Ⓑ plain

● valley

Ⓓ mountain

Name _____

4 What force can rapidly change the Earth's landscape?

Ⓕ wind erosion

Ⓖ weathering

Ⓗ thunderstorms

● volcanic eruptions

5 When igneous rock from a volcanic eruption cools, what does it form?

Ⓐ new core

● new crust

Ⓒ new mantle

Ⓓ new inner core

6 How does water break apart a rock?

Ⓕ It takes up less space when it freezes in cold weather.

Ⓖ It takes up less space when it melts in warm weather.

● It takes up more space when it freezes in cold weather.

Ⓘ It takes up more space when it melts in warm weather.

7 What carries soil away from hilly farm fields?

● rain

Ⓑ plants

Ⓒ rivers

Ⓓ waves

Name _____

8 What causes a rockslide—the quick movement of rocks down a slope?

Ⓕ wind

Ⓖ water

● gravity

Ⓘ glaciers

9 How does erosion **mainly** occur in dry regions?

Ⓐ Gravity pulls soil downhill.

Ⓑ Mud flows quickly down a slope.

● Sand particles blow against rocks.

Ⓓ Rock particles are carried away by water.

10 Look at the illustration below.

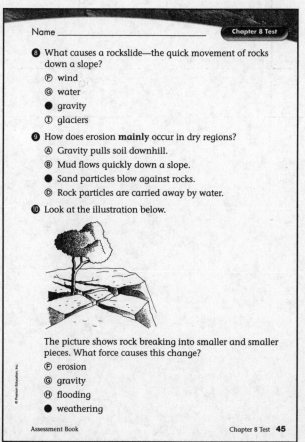

The picture shows rock breaking into smaller and smaller pieces. What force causes this change?

Ⓕ erosion

Ⓖ gravity

Ⓗ flooding

● weathering

Name _____

Write the answers to the questions on the lines.

11 Explain how an earthquake can change Earth's surface. (2 points)

The earthquake's vibrations move as waves that travel back and forth and up and down along Earth's surface. These waves can cause cracks and piles of rubble in landforms near where parts of the crust moved.

12 As a tree grows, it can cause weathering. Explain how the roots of a tree cause weathering. (2 points)

As the roots of a tree grow, they can push through soil and nearby rocks. This pressure can help split the rocks into smaller pieces.

Write the answer to the question on a separate sheet of paper.

13 Earth's surface is constantly changing. Describe how erosion and weathering change Earth's surface. Explain how the processes are alike and different. (4 points)

See page 158 for answer.

Chapter 8 Test

Answer

⓭ Possible answer: Weathering is any action that breaks rocks into smaller pieces. The formations made out of these rocks change shape over a long period of time. Erosion is the movement of weathered material. Both weathering and erosion change landforms over a long period of time. Erosion uses the weathered particles to change the shape of landforms while weathering produces the particles used in erosion.

Intervention and Remediation

⭐ Science Objectives	Test Items	Student Edition Pages	Quick Study Pages	Workbook Pages
The student describes the basic structure of the Earth.	1	222–223	54–55	74
The student knows that landforms change over time (for example, earthquakes, volcanoes).	2, 3, 4, 5, 11	224–229	54–57	74, 75
The student understands the processes of weathering and erosion.	6–10, 12, 13	230–233	58–59	76

Assessment Book

Name _____ **Chapter 9 Test**

Read each question and choose the best answer.
Then fill in the circle next to the correct answer.

1 Important materials from Earth that living things need
   are called
   ● natural resources.
   ⑧ necessary resources.
   © renewable resources.
   ⑩ nonrenewable resources.

2 Which of the following is a nonrenewable resource?
   ● coal
   ⑤ trees
   ⑭ wind
   ① water

3 Choose the term that belongs in the sentence.

   _____ is a resource that cannot be used up.
   ④ Oil
   ⑧ Coal
   © A tree
   ● Sunlight

4 Which of the following is an example of recycling
   a resource?
   ⑥ drinking water instead of milk
   ⑥ adding chocolate sauce to white milk
   ● making a flower pot out of a milk jug
   ① buying milk in quarts instead of gallons

Name _____ **Chapter 9 Test**

5 Look at the illustration below.

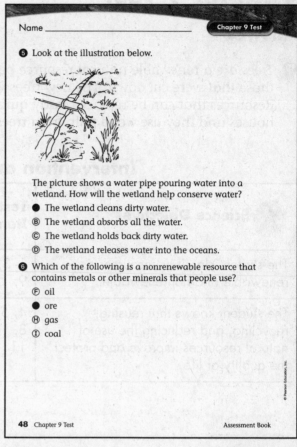

The picture shows a water pipe pouring water into a
wetland. How will the wetland help conserve water?
● The wetland cleans dirty water.
⑧ The wetland absorbs all the water.
© The wetland holds back dirty water.
⑩ The wetland releases water into the oceans.

6 Which of the following is a nonrenewable resource that
   contains metals or other minerals that people use?
   ⑥ oil
   ● ore
   ⑭ gas
   ① coal

Name _____ **Chapter 9 Test**

7 Which of the following makes up **most** of our trash?
   ④ glass
   ● paper
   © plastic
   ⑩ metal cans

8 Using natural resources wisely so we do not waste them is
   called
   ⑥ reusing.
   ⑥ recycling.
   ⑭ containment.
   ● conservation.

9 Look at the illustration below.

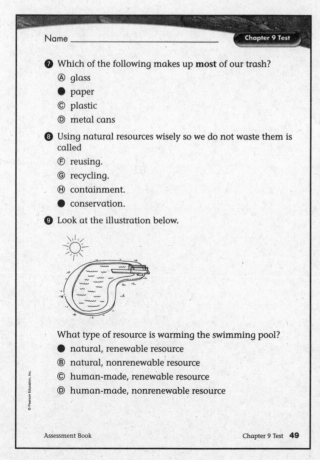

What type of resource is warming the swimming pool?
● natural, renewable resource
⑧ natural, nonrenewable resource
© human-made, renewable resource
⑩ human-made, nonrenewable resource

Name _____ **Chapter 9 Test**

Write the answers to the questions on the lines.

10 Describe two ways that the amount of landfill space can be
    reduced. (2 points)

    People can burn trash in special furnaces and we can create

    less trash to begin with.

11 Identify four things that you can reuse instead of throwing
    away. Explain how you will reuse each item. (2 points)
    Possible answer: I can reuse a plastic water bottle over and

    over, I can donate old clothes that I can't wear anymore, I can

    use a cloth napkin over and over instead of throwing away

    a paper one, I can use plastic bags several times and then

    recycle them instead of throwing them out after one use.

**Write the answer to the question on a separate sheet
of paper.**

12 Trees are an important natural resource.

    Part A Tell if trees are a renewable or nonrenewable
    resource. Explain your answer.

    Part B Name two ways people use trees as a resource.
    (4 points)

    See page 160 for answer.

Chapter 9 Test

Answer

12 Trees are a renewable natural resource because new trees can be planted to replace those that were cut down. The new trees will grow big enough to be cut down again. Resources that can be replaced fairly quickly are renewable. People use trees to build houses and they use wood pulp from trees to make paper and paper products.

Intervention and Remediation

★ Science Objectives	Test Items	Student Edition Pages	Quick Study Pages	Workbook Pages
The student classifies resources as renewable and nonrenewable.	1–3, 6, 9, 12	246–249	60–61	84
The student knows that reusing, recycling, and reducing the use of natural resources improve and protect the quality of life.	4, 5, 7, 8, 10, 11	250–257	62–63, 64–65	85–86

Read each question and choose the best answer.
Then fill in the circle next to the correct answer.

1 A liquid changes into a gas during which process?
Ⓐ melting
● evaporation
Ⓒ precipitation
Ⓓ condensation

2 What type of rock has been changed by heat and/or pressure?
Ⓕ humus rock
Ⓖ igneous rock
Ⓗ sedimentary rock
● metamorphic rock

3 What is the main cause of change to most landforms?
Ⓐ gravity
Ⓑ weathering
Ⓒ erosion by wind
● erosion by water

4 Which of the following is the hardest mineral on Earth?
Ⓕ mica
Ⓖ crocoite
● diamond
Ⓘ molybdenite

---

5 Look at the illustration below.

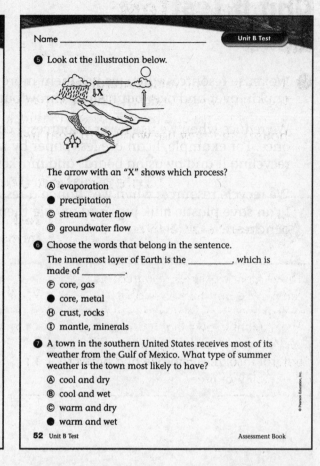

The arrow with an "X" shows which process?
Ⓐ evaporation
● precipitation
Ⓒ stream water flow
Ⓓ groundwater flow

6 Choose the words that belong in the sentence.
The innermost layer of Earth is the _____, which is made of _____.
Ⓕ core, gas
● core, metal
Ⓗ crust, rocks
Ⓘ mantle, minerals

7 A town in the southern United States receives most of its weather from the Gulf of Mexico. What type of summer weather is the town most likely to have?
Ⓐ cool and dry
Ⓑ cool and wet
Ⓒ warm and dry
● warm and wet

---

8 Look at the illustration below.

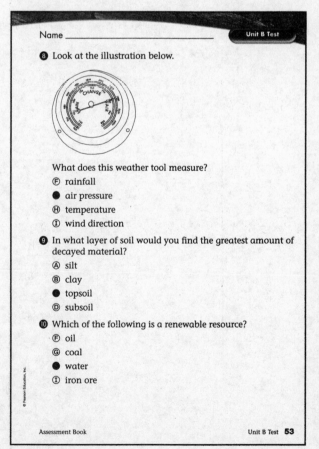

What does this weather tool measure?
Ⓕ rainfall
● air pressure
Ⓗ temperature
Ⓘ wind direction

9 In what layer of soil would you find the greatest amount of decayed material?
Ⓐ silt
Ⓑ clay
● topsoil
Ⓓ subsoil

10 Which of the following is a renewable resource?
Ⓕ oil
Ⓖ coal
● water
Ⓘ iron ore

Write the answers to the questions on the lines.

11 Explain why trees are an important natural resource. Give examples in your answer. (2 points)

Trees are an important natural resource because humans use them for many different things. People use trees to build new houses and make paper and paper products from wood pulp.

12 Volcanoes rapidly change Earth's surface. Describe how a volcano affects Earth's surface. (2 points)

When lava from volcanoes cools on Earth it becomes igneous rock. This is new crust. The lava can build up and form a mountain where there was none before.

Write your answers to the question on a separate sheet of paper.

13 Reusing, reducing, and recycling natural resources are important ways to conserve land and to care for the Earth.

Explain what people do when they reuse, reduce, and recycle natural resources. Then give an example of how you can use each method. (4 points)
See page 162 for answer.

Unit B Test

Answer

13 We reuse resources when we use them more than once. For example, I can use a cloth napkin over and over but I would throw out a paper one.

We reduce when we use fewer resources. I can use fewer items that can be used only once. For example, I can use less paper by using both sides of a sheet of paper before recycling it and by using boards and markers instead of paper.

We recycle resources when we change a resource so it can be used again. For example, I can save plastic milk jugs and recycle them so they can be used to make new park benches.

Unit B Test Talk Answers

Strategy 1   page 56

1. I need to find out why NASA scientists collect information from space about Earth's clouds.
2. I need to find out when students collect information for NASA.
3. I need to find out how clouds are part of the water cycle.

Strategy 2   page 57

1. I found the answer in paragraph 2, sentence 4.
2. I found the answer in paragraph 3, sentence 3.
3. I found the answer in paragraph 2, sentence 3.

Strategy 3   page 58

1. B They want to know how clouds affect Earth's weather.
2. F at assigned times
3. B They work with gases that trap heat and warm Earth.

Strategy 4   page 59

1. **My Notes:** use tools from satellites to collect information about clouds and weather, clouds are part of water cycle, studying how clouds affect Earth's weather
   My Answer: NASA scientists collect information about Earth's clouds using tools on satellites. They use this information to help them study how clouds affect Earth's weather.
2. **My Notes:** interact with gases, trap heat and warm Earth, clouds affect weather
   My Answer: Clouds interact with gases that trap heat and warm the Earth.

Strategy 5   page 60

1. To find the answer, I will find the pictures of cumulus and cirrus clouds and then compare what each type of cloud looks like.
   My Answer: Cumulus clouds are puffy and thick while cirrus clouds are thinner and wispy.
2. To find the answer, I will look at the picture of the stratocumulus cloud and compare it to the cirrus and cumulus cloud pictures.
   My Answer: A stratocumulus cloud gets its name from having features that look like both the stratus clouds and the cumulus clouds.

Strategy 6   page 61

1. To score higher, Dylan needs to take out the information about the weather cycle and weather occurring in the world. Dylan could also add a line about how NASA scientists use the information collected to study clouds.
2. To score higher, Lakeisha needs to take out the information about students recording information about precipitation, since that is not mentioned in the text. She also needs to clarify that students take their measurements at given times, so that their measurements occur at the same time when tools on the NASA satellite are recording information in the area.

Unit B Writing Prompt

Describe the forces that change Earth's surface. In your description, include forces that quickly change Earth's surface and forces that slowly change Earth's surface.

Grade 3 Writing Scoring Guide [Use with Unit B]

Score	Focus	Organization	Support	Conventions	Science Content
6	well focused on the topic	logical organizational pattern with a beginning, middle, and conclusion; excellent use of transitional devices	ample development of the supporting ideas, demonstrates a sense of completeness or wholeness; precision in word choice	generally correct subject/verb agreement and verb and noun forms; complete sentences except when fragments are used purposefully; a variety of sentence structures	no errors
5	focused on the topic	organizational pattern with a few lapses; good use of transitional devices	adequate development of the supporting ideas with a sense of completeness or wholeness; adequate word choice but may lack precision	occasional errors in subject/verb agreement and in standard forms of verbs and nouns, but not enough to impede communication; generally follows conventions of punctuation, capitalization, and spelling; most sentences complete; some variety of sentence structures	few errors
4	fairly well focused on the topic but some loosely related information	evidence of an organizational pattern and transitional devices, but with some lapses	supporting ideas contain details but sometimes not developed; generally adequate word choice	demonstrates knowledge of conventions of punctuation and capitalization; correct spelling of commonly used words; an attempt to use a variety of sentence structures, although some are simple	some minor errors
3	generally focused on the topic but some extraneous information	organizational pattern attempted with some transitional devices, but some lapses	some supporting ideas not developed with details; adequate but limited word choice; occasionally vague	demonstrates knowledge of conventions of punctuation and capitalization, but some errors; correct spelling of commonly used words; an attempt to use a variety of sentence structures, although most are simple	1 or 2 significant errors
2	slightly related to topic	little evidence of an organizational pattern or transitional devices	development of supporting ideas often inadequate or illogical; limited or immature word choice	frequent errors in basic punctuation and capitalization; commonly used words frequently misspelled; primarily simple sentence constructions	significant errors
1	minimally addresses the topic	does not exhibit an organizational pattern	little, if any, development of supporting ideas, and usually provided through lists, clichés, and limited or immature word choice	frequent errors in spelling, capitalization, punctuation, and sentence structure; sentences primarily simple constructions	gross errors

Unscorable: The response has one or more of these problems: the response is not related to what the prompt requested the student to do; the response is simply a rewording of the prompt; the response is a copy of a published work; the student refused to write; the response is written in a foreign language; the response is illegible; the response is incomprehensible (words are arranged in such a way that no meaning is conveyed)

Assessment Book

Grade 3

Anchor Paper: 6 points

Describe the forces that change Earth's surface. In your description, include forces that quickly change Earth's surface and forces that slowly change Earth's surface.

Earth's surface is always changing through both rapid and slow forces. Volcanoes and earthquakes cause quick changes in Earth's surface and erosion and weathering cause slow changes in Earth's surface.

When a volcano erupts hot, melted rock called lava flows out. As the lava cools it hardens and turns into igneous rock. Where the lava forms rock, Earth has a brand new crust. During an earthquake, the shifts in Earth's crust case the ground to vibrate in many directions. These vibrations move up and down and back and forth along Earth's surface and can cause cracks and tumbled piles in landforms.

Weathering is constantly changing Earth's surface. Any time larger rock is broken into smaller pieces, the rock has weathered. Freezing and thawing water, moving glaciers, worms digging through soil, and tree roots all cause weathering. Erosion is the movement of weathered material. Wind, water, glaciers, and gravity carry particles that then bump against rocks and break off grains.

The surface of Earth is in a constant state of change. Some changes are so slow we cannot tell them from day to day and other changes happen so quickly, we can easily view the changes.

Score Point: 6

The writing focuses well on the topic. The organization has a beginning, middle, and conclusion with excellent use of transitional devices. The writing exhibits ample development of supporting ideas, demonstrates a sense of completeness or wholeness and a precision in word choice. Grammar usage is generally correct with subject/verb agreement and proper verb and noun forms. The paper is written in complete sentences except when fragments are used purposefully and there is variety in sentence structures. There are no errors in content.

Anchor Paper: 5 points

Describe the forces that change Earth's surface. In your description, include forces that quickly change Earth's surface and forces that slowly change Earth's surface.

Earth's surface is always changing. Some changes happen quickly, while others take a long time. Volcanoes and earthquakes cause quick changes in Earth's surface and erosion and weathering cause slow changes in Earth's surface.

When a volcano erupts hot rock flows out. As the lava cools it turns into new rock. Where the lava forms rock Earth has a new crust. During an earthquake, the shifts in Earth's crust cause the ground to shake. These vibrations along Earth's surface and can cause cracks and tumbled piles in landforms.

Weathering is always changing Earth's surface. When a larger rock is broken into smaller pieces, the rock has weathered. Many things cause weathering. Freezing and thawing water, moving glaciers, worms digging through soil, and tree roots all cause weathering. Erosion is the movement of weathered material. Wind, water, glaciers, and gravity carry particles that then bump against rocks and break of grains.

The surface of Earth is in a constant state of change. Some changes are so slow we cannot see them and others are very fast.

Score Point: 5

The writing is focused on the topic. The paper is organized with only a few lapses and has good transitional devices. The writing is adequately developed, uses supporting ideas with a sense of completeness or wholeness. The word choice is adequate but may lack precision. There are occasional errors in subject/verb agreement and in standard forms of verbs and nouns, but not enough to impede communication. The conventions of punctuation, capitalization, and spelling are generally followed. Most sentences are complete and there is some variety of sentence structures. There are a few errors in content.

Grade 3

Describe the forces that change Earth's surface. In your description, include forces that quickly change Earth's surface and forces that slowly change Earth's surface.

Earth's surface is always changing. Some changes happen quickly, while others take a long time.

Volcanoes and earthquakes quickly change Earth's surface. When a volcano erupts hot rock flows out. Where the lava cools Earth has a new crust. During an earthquake, the shifts in Earth's crust case the ground to shake. This shakes Earth's surface and can cause cracks and tumbled piles in landforms. Earthquakes also damage buildings and roadways.

Weathering is always changing Earth's surface. When a larger rock is broken into smaller pieces, the rock has weathered. Many things cause weathering. Freezing and thawing water, moving glaciers, worms digging through soil, and tree roots all cause weathering. Erosion is the movement of weathered material. Erosion happens everywhere. In the desert, sand is the main cause of erosion.

The surface of Earth is always changing, sometimes slowly, sometimes quickly.

Score Point: 4

The writing focuses fairly well on the topic but contains some loosely related information. The paper shows evidence of an organizational pattern and transitional devices but has some lapses. The supporting ideas, while sometimes containing specifics and details, are sometimes also not developed. The word choice is generally adequate. The writing demonstrates knowledge of conventions of punctuation and capitalization and correct spelling of commonly used words. There is an attempt to use a variety of sentence structures, although some are simple. There are some minor errors in content.

Grade 3

Anchor Paper: 3 points

Describe the forces that change Earth's surface. In your description, include forces that quickly change Earth's surface and forces that slowly change Earth's surface.

Earth's surface is always changing. Some changes happen quickly, while others take a long time.

Volcanos and earthquakes change Earth's surface. Volcanos shot out hot rock. Where the lava cools it destroys the Earth's old surface. During an earthquake, Earth's surface shakes mountains, buildings, roadways, and other things. These things can tumble down.

Weathering is when a large rock is broken into small pieces. Freezing and thawing water cause weathering. Erasion is pieces of sand and other little things carried by the wind and then hitting other objects. Erasion happens everywhere.

Score Point: 3

The writing generally focuses on the topic but has some extraneous information. The paper shows an organizational pattern with some attempts to use transitional devices but some lapses occur. There are some supporting ideas but they are not developed with specifics and details. Word choice is adequate but limited and occasionally vague. The writing demonstrates knowledge of conventions of punctuation and capitalization but has some errors. Commonly used words are correctly spelled. An attempt is made to use a variety of sentence structures, although most are simple. There are 1 or 2 significant errors in content.

© Pearson Education, Inc.

Grade 3

Anchor Paper: 2 points

Describe the forces that change Earth's surface. In your description, include forces that quickly change Earth's surface and forces that slowly change Earth's surface.

Earth's surface changes, sometimes quickley sometimes slowely.

Volcanos change Earth's surface. Lava flows out and makes rocks. Weathering is when a larg rock is broken into littel pieces. Erasion is peices of sand and other little things carried by the wind and then hitting other objects. Erasion happens all the time.

Score Point: 2

The writing is slightly related to the topic. There is little evidence of an organizational pattern or use of transitional devices. The development of supporting ideas is often inadequate or illogical. Word choice is limited or immature. The paper has frequent errors in basic punctuation and capitalization. Commonly used words are frequently misspelled. Sentence constructions are primarily simple. There are significant errors in content.

Grade 3

Anchor Paper: 1 point

Describe the forces that change Earth's surface. In your description, include forces that quickly change Earth's surface and forces that slowly change Earth's surface.

Earth surface always changes. Volcanos changes Earths surface. Volcanos makes rocks. Weathering makes big rocks into littel rocks. Airoshun is pieces of sand. And other littel things in wind and then hitting things. This happuns all the time.

Score Point: 1

The writing minimally addresses the topic and does not exhibit an organizational pattern. There are little, if any, supporting ideas and those ideas are usually provided through lists, clichés, and limited or immature word choice. The writing shows frequent errors in spelling, capitalization, punctuation, and sentence structure. Sentences are primarily simple constructions. There are gross errors in content.

Unit B Performance Test Instructions

Classifying Trash

Description: Students are asked to group items in a trash bag as reusable, recyclable, or capable of being converted to mulch; to find the mass of a trash bag and the mass of recyclable, not recyclable, and plant material that make up the trash; and to describe ways reusable and recyclable items can be reused.

Purpose: To evaluate a student's ability to classify information and draw conclusions about reducing, reusing, and recycling materials based on the student's classification of trash.

Science Process Skill: Classifying

Time: Stations 1, 2, and 3 are designed to take students 35–40 minutes to complete.

Teacher Instructions

Station 1
Materials
> paper bag
> an assortment of trash items such as:

aluminum foil	baby food jar
plastic straw	metal jar lid
craft stick	paper napkin
foam cup	plastic sandwich bag
piece of string	tree leaf
aluminum can	plant stem
crumpled sheet of white paper	old potato

> Blackline Masters: pages 63 and 173

Preparation

1. Make copies of the blackline masters. Page 173 provides station setup instructions. Students can use page 63 to record their answers.

2. Check items for sharp edges, points, and so on. Remove any unsafe items.

3. Use an assortment of clean paper, plastic, metal, glass, and plant items.

Teaching Tips

- The types of materials accepted as recyclable may differ from community to community.

- Alert students to the presence of the recyclable logo on items.

Station 2
Materials
    pan balance and set of masses
    paper bag
    an assortment of trash items such as:

aluminum foil	baby food jar
plastic straw	metal jar lid
craft stick	paper napkin
foam cup	plastic sandwich bag
piece of string	tree leaf
aluminum can	plant stem
crumpled sheet of white paper	old potato

    Blackline Masters: pages 63 and 173

Preparation
1. Use page 173 to provide station setup instructions. Students can use page 63 to record their answers.
2. Check items for sharp edges, points, and so on. Remove any unsafe items.
3. Check periodically to make sure that the pans of the balance are balanced.
4. For your own reference, find the mass of the bag of trash, the mass of the recyclable materials, the mass of the materials that are not recyclable, and the mass of the plant material.

Teaching Tip
• Make sure students include the paper bag in their assessment.

Station 3
Materials
    paper bag
    an assortment of trash items such as:

aluminum foil	baby food jar
plastic straw	metal jar lid
craft stick	paper napkin
foam cup	plastic sandwich bag
piece of string	tree leaf
aluminum can	plant stem
crumpled sheet of white paper	old potato

    Blackline Masters: pages 64 and 174

Preparation
1. Make copies of the blackline masters. Page 174 provides station setup instructions. Students can use page 64 to record their answers.
2. Check items for sharp edges, points, and so on. Remove any unsafe items.

Station 1

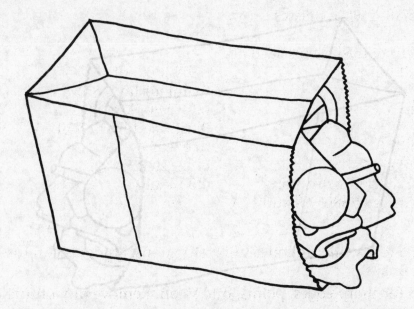

Be sure that the materials are set up like this before you leave this station.

Station 2

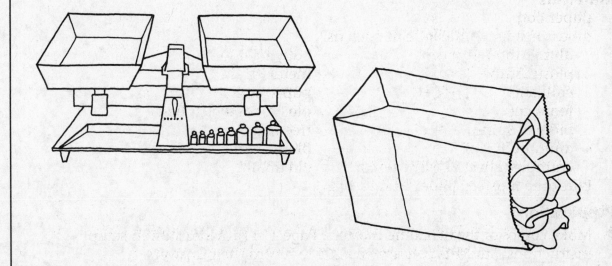

Be sure that the materials are set up like this before you leave this station.

Station 3

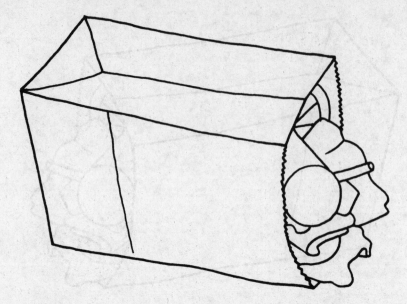

Be sure that the materials are set up like this before you leave this station.

Scoring Guide

Station 1

3 points Student records a classification system relating to reducing, reusing, or recycling trash and lists items in each category.

2 points Student records a classification system relating to reducing, reusing, or recycling trash but does not list items.

1 point Student needs assistance to develop a classification system relating to reducing, reusing, or recycling trash.

Station 2

3 points Student finds and records the total mass of trash and the mass for each category of items that makes up the trash.

2 points Student partially accomplishes the tasks of finding and recording masses.

1 point Student needs assistance finding and recording masses.

Station 3

3 points Student identifies three reusable items and describes ways to reuse them.

2 points Student identifies two reusable items and describes ways to reuse them.

1 point Student needs assistance to either identify reusable items or to describe ways to reuse them.

Data Analysis

3 points Student records two or more ways to reduce, reuse, and recycle trash.

2 points Student records one way to reduce, reuse, and recycle trash.

1 point Student needs assistance to identify a way to reduce, reuse, and recycle trash.

Total Score

Points	Percent equivalent
12	100
11	92
10	83
9	75
8	67
7	58
6	50
5	42
4	33
3	25
2	16
1	8

Classifying Trash

Your assignment is to prepare a television news report describing how everyone can reduce, reuse, and recycle.

Station 1

Use the card at the station to correctly set up the equipment.

Trash Classification

Decide which items in the bag of trash could be reused, recycled, or used as mulch. List the items in each category.

Accept all reasonable classification systems that are devised by

students.

Station 2

Use the card at the station to correctly set up the equipment.

Trash Measurement

Find the mass of the entire bag of trash. Then sort the trash into three piles: recyclable, not recyclable, and plant material. Find the mass of each pile.

Masses			
Total	Recyclable	Not Recyclable	Plant Material
Check mass given.	**Check mass given.**	**Check mass given.**	**Check mass given.**

Station 3

Use the card at the station to correctly set up the equipment.

Reuse Suggestions

For three items you classified as reusable or recyclable, describe a way that each item could be reused.

Check students' descriptions and drawings based on materials in

the bag. For example, a crumpled sheet of white paper could be

recycled to make more paper or a baby food jar could be reused

as a container for paper clips.

Data Analysis

You have completed your study of the trash. Use the data you have collected and what you know about conservation to answer the following questions.

What would you say on the television news report about ways to reduce, reuse, and recycle trash? What would you say about using plant materials to make compost?

Student responses should include information from all three

stations that were used in the performance test. Student answers

should indicate that reducing, reusing, and recycling materials

greatly decreases the amount of trash that is produced. Further,

plant materials can be reused as compost to enrich the soil,

rather than just rotting in trash containers.

Read each question and choose the best answer.
Then fill in the circle next to the correct answer.

1 Which of the following **best** describes matter?

Ⓐ anything that is made of only one element

● anything that takes up space and has mass

Ⓒ anything that is found on the periodic table

Ⓓ anything that you can observe with your senses

2 A scientist describes an object as small, shiny, and bumpy. The scientist is observing the object's _____.

Ⓕ senses

Ⓖ density

Ⓗ volume

● properties

3 What type of matter is made of particles that are tightly packed together and firmly connected?

Ⓐ gas

● solid

Ⓒ liquid

Ⓓ plasma

4 How is a gas different from a solid or liquid?

Ⓕ A gas has a certain shape that does not change.

Ⓖ A gas changes shape over a long period of time.

● A gas spreads out to fill whatever space is available.

Ⓘ A gas has a tightly packed shape, but jiggles very quickly.

---

5 How are elements organized in the periodic table?

Ⓐ They are organized by their individual shapes.

Ⓑ They are organized by the mass of each element.

● They are organized by their individual properties.

Ⓓ They are organized by the volume of each element.

6 Which choice below **best** completes the sentence? _____ is the smallest particle of an element that has the properties of that element.

Ⓕ a solid

Ⓖ a gram

● an atom

Ⓘ an ounce

7 Look at the illustration below.

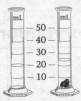

What is the volume of the rock?

Ⓐ 1 mL

● 5 mL

Ⓒ 25 mL

Ⓓ You cannot tell from the picture.

---

8 How is mass different from weight?

Ⓕ Mass is different in different places.

Ⓖ Mass is measured in ounces and pounds.

Ⓗ Mass changes from Earth to the Moon.

● Mass remains the same no matter where the object is.

9 A golfer hits a ball into a pond. The ball sinks in the pond. What does this tell the golfer about the golf ball?

● The golf ball had little buoyancy.

Ⓑ The golf ball had a lot of buoyancy.

Ⓒ The golf ball is less dense than the water.

Ⓓ The golf ball must have had cork in the middle.

10 Which of the following is **best** measured with kilometers?

Ⓕ the length of a pencil

Ⓖ the height of a student

Ⓗ the length of a classroom

● the distance from one city to another

11 How can you measure the volume of a box?

Ⓐ Use a balance.

● See how many cubes of a known size fit inside the box.

Ⓒ Use a hand lens to see the small markings on a metric ruler.

Ⓓ Compare the mass of the box with the mass of a standard box of the same size.

Write the answer to the question on the lines.

12 Look at the illustration below.

Describe the object's properties. Tell about a tool you could use to observe the object in more detail. (2 points)

The ball is generally round and it has lots of pointy bumps

that look like little pyramids all around it. I could use a hand

lens to see more detail.

Write the answers to the question on a separate sheet of paper.

13 A student finds a small, unknown object during a recent scientific dig.

Part A Explain how the student can find the mass of the object. Include in your answer the units used to record the mass.

Part B Describe how the student can find the volume of the object. Include in your answer the units used to record the volume. (4 points)

See page 178 for answer.

Chapter 10 Test

Answer

⓭ The student can find the mass by using a balance. The student can place the object on one side and the known masses on the other. When the object and masses are level, the student can find the mass of the object by adding the known masses needed to balance it. The mass will probably be in grams since the object is small.

The student can find the volume by using a measuring cup. The student can put water into the cup and record the level, and then put the object into the cup and record the level. The difference between the water levels is the volume. The volume will probably be in milliliters since the object is small.

Intervention and Remediation

★ Science Objectives	Test Items	Student Edition Pages	Quick Study Pages	Workbook Pages
The student observes and describes the properties of matter.	1, 2, 12	278–279	66–67	94
The student compares and contrasts the forms of matter.	3, 4	280–281	66–67	94
The student explains the makeup of matter.	5, 6	282–283	66–67	94
The student determines the physical properties of matter using metric measurements that incorporate tools such as rulers, thermometers, balances.	7–11, 13	284–289	68–69	95

Name _____

Read each question and choose the best answer.
Then fill in the circle next to the correct answer.

1 Which of the following is a physical change?
- ● cutting fruit
- Ⓑ cooking eggs
- Ⓒ rusting metal
- Ⓓ burning wood

2 Choose the words that belong in the sentence.
When water changes from a liquid to a solid, it _____,
which is a _____ change.
- Ⓕ melts, physical
- Ⓖ melts, chemical
- ● freezes, physical
- Ⓘ freezes, chemical

3 Why is lemonade a solution?
- Ⓐ It is one substance whose kind of matter is changed.
- Ⓑ It is one substance whose kind of matter is not changed.
- Ⓒ It is a combination of two or more substances and a new kind of matter is made.
- ● It is a combination of two or more substances and the kind of matter of each is not changed.

Assessment Book

Name _____

4 Look at the illustration below. Complete the sentence.

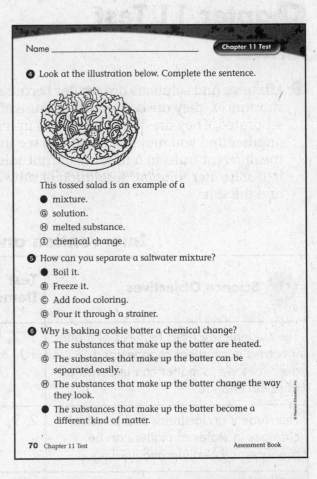

This tossed salad is an example of a
- ● mixture.
- Ⓖ solution.
- Ⓗ melted substance.
- Ⓘ chemical change.

5 How can you separate a saltwater mixture?
- ● Boil it.
- Ⓑ Freeze it.
- Ⓒ Add food coloring.
- Ⓓ Pour it through a strainer.

6 Why is baking cookie batter a chemical change?
- Ⓕ The substances that make up the batter are heated.
- Ⓖ The substances that make up the batter can be separated easily.
- Ⓗ The substances that make up the batter change the way they look.
- ● The substances that make up the batter become a different kind of matter.

Assessment Book

Name _____

7 Look at the illustration below.

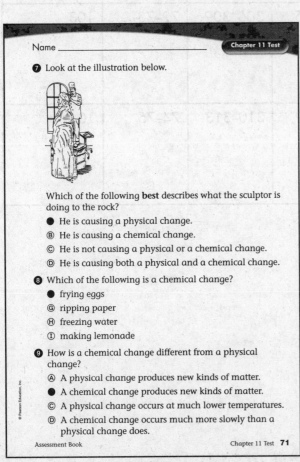

Which of the following **best** describes what the sculptor is doing to the rock?
- ● He is causing a physical change.
- Ⓑ He is causing a chemical change.
- Ⓒ He is not causing a physical or a chemical change.
- Ⓓ He is causing both a physical and a chemical change.

8 Which of the following is a chemical change?
- ● frying eggs
- Ⓖ ripping paper
- Ⓗ freezing water
- Ⓘ making lemonade

9 How is a chemical change different from a physical change?
- Ⓐ A physical change produces new kinds of matter.
- ● A chemical change produces new kinds of matter.
- Ⓒ A physical change occurs at much lower temperatures.
- Ⓓ A chemical change occurs much more slowly than a physical change does.

Assessment Book

Name _____

Write the answers to the questions on the lines.

10 Identify four ways that physical changes can occur in matter. (2 points)

Possible answers: Matter can be heated or cooled, it can be

cut into pieces, it can be stretched or folded.

11 Explain how chemical changes help you use a battery-operated cell phone. (2 points)

When I use the cell phone, the chemicals combine inside

batteries. This causes new substances to form. The chemical

change releases electricity to power the cell phone.

Write the answer to the question on a separate sheet of paper.

12 How are mixtures and solutions similar? How are they different? Give examples. (4 points)
See page 180 for answer.

Assessment Book

Assessment Book

Chapter 11 Test

Answer

⑫ Mixtures and solutions are similar because they are both made of two or more substances, they are both made because of a physical change, and they both can be separated. They are different because in a solution one or more substances dissolves in another and you may not be able to see the particles. For example, you can easily see the different fruits in a mixture of fruit salad but you cannot see the small salt particles in a saltwater solution. A solution of saltwater must be boiled to separate the water and the salt.

Intervention and Remediation

★ Science Objectives	Test Items	Student Edition Pages	Quick Study Pages	Workbook Pages
The student describes features of matter involved in physical changes and describes ways matter can undergo a physical change.	1, 7, 9, 10	302–305	70–71	102
The student understands that physical changes in states of matter can be produced by heating and cooling.	2, 9, 10	302–305	70–71	102
The student knows that different materials are made by physically combining substances and that different objects can be made by combining different materials.	3, 4, 5, 12	306–309	72–73	103
The student knows that different materials made by chemically combining two or more substances may have properties that differ from the original materials.	6, 8, 9, 11	310–313	74–75	104

Read each question and choose the best answer.
Then fill in the circle next to the correct answer.

1 How would you best describe the motion of a Ferris wheel?

Ⓐ wave

● circular

Ⓒ forward

Ⓓ backward

2 Choose the words that belong in the sentence.

If a stoplight is in front of the car and then behind the car, the _____ of the stoplight has changed.

Ⓕ relative motion

Ⓖ circular motion

● relative position

Ⓘ circular position

3 A bicyclist travels at 8 mph, 12 mph, 9 mph, and 15 mph. How can you **best** describe the bicyclist's speed?

Ⓐ fast

Ⓑ slow

● variable

Ⓓ constant

4 If the same amount of force is applied to each box below, which box will move the greatest distance?

● 7 kg box

Ⓖ 12 kg box

Ⓗ 23 kg box

Ⓘ 100 kg box

---

5 Which surface produces the least amount of friction?

Ⓐ rocky gravel road

Ⓑ grassy soccer field

Ⓒ bumpy new carpet

● smooth ceramic tile

6 Look at the illustration below.

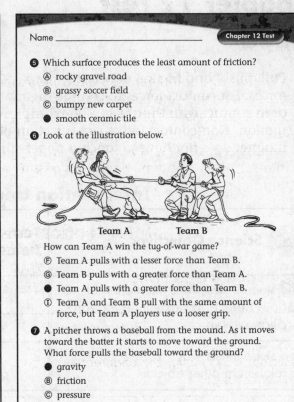

Team A   Team B

How can Team A win the tug-of-war game?

Ⓕ Team A pulls with a lesser force than Team B.

Ⓖ Team B pulls with a greater force than Team A.

● Team A pulls with a greater force than Team B.

Ⓘ Team A and Team B pull with the same amount of force, but Team A players use a looser grip.

7 A pitcher throws a baseball from the mound. As it moves toward the batter it starts to move toward the ground. What force pulls the baseball toward the ground?

● gravity

Ⓑ friction

Ⓒ pressure

Ⓓ magnetism

---

8 Which of the following is an example of work?

● kicking a ball downhill

Ⓖ thinking about homework

Ⓗ holding the ball before winding up for a pitch

Ⓘ pushing against a concrete pillar with all your might

9 Which tool is a wedge?

● axe

Ⓑ ramp

Ⓒ jar lid

Ⓓ doorknob

10 Look at the illustration below.

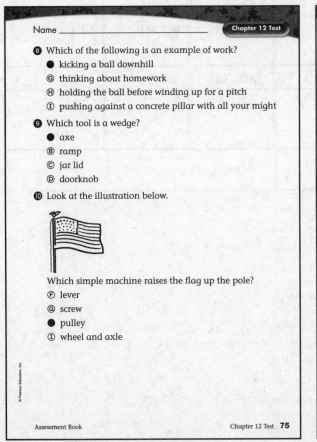

Which simple machine raises the flag up the pole?

Ⓕ lever

Ⓖ screw

● pulley

Ⓘ wheel and axle

Write the answers to the questions on the lines.

11 Describe two ways gravity can affect the movement of a wheel and axle in a bicycle. (2 points)

Gravity can make it harder to move a wheel forward going

uphill and easier to move the wheel going downhill. You have

to apply more force to the pedals going uphill and less force

going downhill.

12 How do simple machines make work easier? (2 points)

Simple machines help people do the work with less force, but

they don't lessen the amount of work.

Write your answer to the question on a separate sheet of paper.

13 *Part A* Identify three contact forces and two non-contact forces.

Part B Explain how contact forces are different from non-contact forces. Give examples to support your answer. (4 points)

See page 182 for answer.

© Pearson Education, Inc.

Assessment Book   **Answer Key   181**

Chapter 12 Test

Answer

⑬ Pull, push, and friction are contact forces. Gravity and magnetism are non-contact forces. For contact forces to change the motion of an object, they need to be touching or in contact with the object. For example, a bat needs to hit a ball to change its motion. Non-contact forces can affect an object without touching it. For example, a magnet does not have to touch a paper clip to attract it.

Intervention and Remediation

★ Science Objectives	Test Items	Student Edition Pages	Quick Study Pages	Workbook Pages
The student describes the motion of various objects (for example, forward, circular, wave).	1	326–327	76–77	112
The student lists ways to view objects in relation to other objects.	2	328–329	76–77	112
The student knows that an object may move in a straight line at a constant speed, speed up, slow down, or change direction dependent on net force acting on the object.	3, 4, 5, 6, 7, 13	330–337	76–79	112, 113
The student explains how forces can be harnessed to perform work.	8, 11, 12	338–343	80–81	114
The student knows the six types of simple machines (screw, inclined plane, wedge, pulley, lever, and wheel and axle).	9, 10	340–343	80–81	114

Name _____

**Read each question and choose the best answer.
Then fill in the circle next to the correct answer.**

1 Complete the sentence.
The Sun's energy reaches Earth as _____.
- ● heat energy and light energy
- Ⓑ kinetic energy and light energy
- Ⓒ kinetic energy and chemical energy
- Ⓓ electrical energy and chemical energy

2 What happens when we burn fuels such as coal and gasoline?
- Ⓕ We change heat energy to light energy to do work.
- Ⓖ We change kinetic energy to heat energy to do work.
- ● We release the potential energy within them to do work.
- Ⓘ We release the electrical energy within them to do work.

3 Which of these objects has kinetic energy?
- Ⓐ car moving on a road
- Ⓑ skier going down a slope
- Ⓒ ball rolling down a ramp
- ● all of the above.

4 What happens to the chemical energy in the battery when you use an electric toothbrush?
- Ⓕ It changes into kinetic energy and then potential energy.
- Ⓖ It changes into potential energy and then kinetic energy.
- ● It changes into electrical energy and then kinetic energy.
- Ⓘ It changes into kinetic energy and then electrical energy.

Name _____

5 What is an electric circuit?
- Ⓐ the movement of electric energy
- Ⓑ an outlet you can plug a cord into
- ● the path that an electric current flows through
- Ⓓ a machine used to change sunlight into electricity

6 What is the trough of a wave?
- Ⓕ the top of the wave
- Ⓖ the width of the wave
- Ⓗ the length of the wave
- ● the bottom of the wave

7 What happens when a warm object comes into contact with a cool object?
- Ⓐ The cool object loses heat.
- Ⓑ The warm object gains heat.
- ● The warm object loses heat and the cool one gains heat.
- Ⓓ The cool object loses heat and the warm one gains heat.

8 When can you notice friction?
- Ⓕ when wood burns
- Ⓖ when sunlight warms the sand at a beach
- Ⓗ when you heat frozen vegetables in a pot on the stove
- ● when you warm your hands by rubbing them together

Name _____

9 How does heat make liquid water change?
- Ⓐ The liquid water becomes ice.
- Ⓑ The liquid water becomes a solid.
- Ⓒ The liquid water evaporates and disappears.
- ● The liquid water evaporates and becomes a gas.

10 What is a chemical change that gives off light and heat?
- Ⓕ boiling
- ● burning
- Ⓗ freezing
- Ⓘ evaporating

11 Look at the illustration.

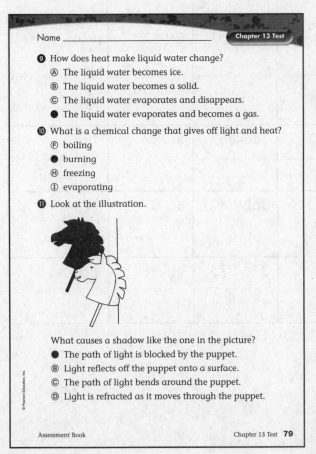

What causes a shadow like the one in the picture?
- ● The path of light is blocked by the puppet.
- Ⓑ Light reflects off the puppet onto a surface.
- Ⓒ The path of light bends around the puppet.
- Ⓓ Light is refracted as it moves through the puppet.

Name _____

12 How does the lens in a telescope make objects appear larger?
- Ⓕ It reflects light.
- ● It refracts light.
- Ⓗ It absorbs light.
- Ⓘ It separates light.

Write the answers to the questions on the lines.

13 Why will paper stick to a balloon that you have rubbed on your hair? (2 points)

The balloon picks up negative charges from the hair. The

extra negative charge on the balloon is attracted to the

positive charge of the paper.

14 What are two ways that energy can travel from one place to another? (2 points)

Energy can be carried by a moving object, and it can travel in

waves.

Write your answer to the question on a separate sheet of paper.

15 Name three main sources of light and give examples of each. (4 points)
See page 184 for answer.

Assessment Book

Answer Key **183**

Chapter 13 Test

Answer

⑮ The Sun is our main source of light. Its light travels in waves. Chemical changes like burning wood or candles are another source. Electricity makes the wire in a light bulb get so hot it glows, giving off light.

Intervention and Remediation

★ Science Objectives	Test Items	Student Edition Pages	Quick Study Pages	Workbook Pages
The student knows that the Sun provides energy for the Earth in the form of heat and light.	1	358–359	82–83	122
The student knows examples of potential and kinetic energy.	2, 3	360–361	82–83	122
The student understands the characteristics of waves.	6, 14	364–365	84–85	123
The student knows different forms of energy and ways to measure amounts of energy that are transformed from one form of energy to another.	4, 5, 11, 12, 15	362–363, 370–373, 376–377	84–85, 88–89, 90–91	123, 125, 126
The student knows that when a warmer object comes in contact with a cooler one, the warm object loses heat and the cool one gains it until they are both the same temprature.	7	366–367	86–87	124
The student knows ways that heat can be produced by chemical reactions, electrical machines, and friction.	8, 10	366–367	86–87	124
The student understands that changes in states of matter relate to changes in temperature.	9	368–369	86–87	124
The student understands static electricity in terms of attraction and repulsion.	13	374–375	90–91	126

Name _____

**Read each question and choose the best answer.
Then fill in the circle next to the correct answer.**

❶ Which of the following is true about sound?

Ⓐ All sounds are loud.

● All sounds are made when matter moves.

Ⓒ Some sounds are so loud you cannot hear them.

Ⓓ Some sounds are made when matter moves and some are made when matter rests.

❷ Matter moving back and forth quickly is called

Ⓕ pitch.

● vibration.

Ⓗ a soft sound.

Ⓘ a loud sound.

❸ Hitting a tambourine with less force will make the sound

● softer.

Ⓑ louder.

Ⓒ higher in pitch.

Ⓓ higher in vibration.

❹ How do wind instruments make sound?

● Air inside them vibrates.

Ⓖ Reeds inside them vibrate.

Ⓗ Someone hits the instrument.

Ⓘ Someone presses valves on the instrument.

© Pearson Education, Inc.

Name _____

❺ Look at the illustration below.

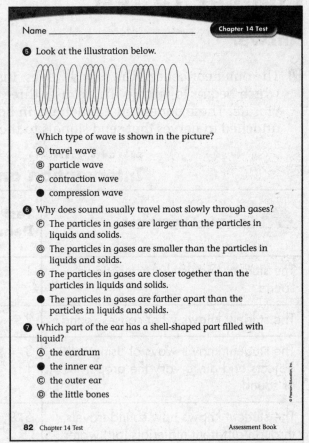

Which type of wave is shown in the picture?

Ⓐ travel wave

Ⓑ particle wave

Ⓒ contraction wave

● compression wave

❻ Why does sound usually travel most slowly through gases?

Ⓕ The particles in gases are larger than the particles in liquids and solids.

Ⓖ The particles in gases are smaller than the particles in liquids and solids.

Ⓗ The particles in gases are closer together than the particles in liquids and solids.

● The particles in gases are farther apart than the particles in liquids and solids.

❼ Which part of the ear has a shell-shaped part filled with liquid?

Ⓐ the eardrum

● the inner ear

Ⓒ the outer ear

Ⓓ the little bones

© Pearson Education, Inc.

Name _____

❽ Look at the illustration below.

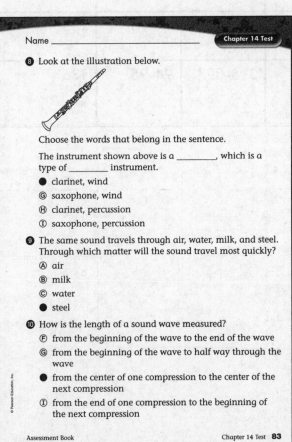

Choose the words that belong in the sentence.

The instrument shown above is a _____, which is a type of _____ instrument.

● clarinet, wind

Ⓖ saxophone, wind

Ⓗ clarinet, percussion

Ⓘ saxophone, percussion

❾ The same sound travels through air, water, milk, and steel. Through which matter will the sound travel most quickly?

Ⓐ air

Ⓑ milk

Ⓒ water

● steel

❿ How is the length of a sound wave measured?

Ⓕ from the beginning of the wave to the end of the wave

Ⓖ from the beginning of the wave to half way through the wave

● from the center of one compression to the center of the next compression

Ⓘ from the end of one compression to the beginning of the next compression

© Pearson Education, Inc.

Name _____

Write the answers to the questions on the lines.

⓫ A student says that an object that vibrates more quickly has a lower pitch. Is the student correct? Explain your reasoning. (2 points)

The student is incorrect. An object that vibrates more quickly

has a higher pitch than an object that vibrates more slowly.

The student should say an object that vibrates more quickly

has a higher pitch.

⓬ Sound travels in waves. Compare the speeds at which sound waves travel as they go through air, water, and solids. Also explain why the speeds are different. (2 points)

Sound waves usually travel most quickly through solids and

most slowly through air. The reason for this is that particles in

air are farther apart than particles in solids. Therefore, since

sound waves travel through particles, it takes them longer

to travel through air than it does for them to travel through a

solid.

Write your answer to the question on a separate sheet of paper.

⓭ Describe how sound waves travel through human ears to the brain. (4 points)

See page 186 for answer.

© Pearson Education, Inc.

Chapter 14 Test

Answer

⑬ The outer ear collects the sound waves. Inside the ear the waves hit the eardrum, which begins to vibrate. This causes three tiny bones attached to the eardrum to vibrate. These bones cause tiny hairs in liquid in the inner ear to vibrate. The hairs are attached to nerves that send signals to the brain.

Intervention and Remediation

⭐ Science Objectives	Test Items	Student Edition Pages	Quick Study Pages	Workbook Pages
The student knows characteristics of sound.	1	390–391	92–93	134
The student knows what causes sound.	2	392–393	92–93	134
The student knows ways of using solid objects and air to vary the properties of sound.	3, 4, 8, 11	392–395	92–93	134
The student knows how sound travels through different materials (air, water, solids).	6, 9, 12	398–399	94–95	135
The student knows the ear is the receiver of sound vibrations.	7, 13	400–401	94–95	135
The student understands the characteristics of waves (for example, crest, trough, length).	5, 10	396–397	94–95	135

**Read each question and choose the best answer.
Then fill in the circle next to the correct answer.**

1 A student pours 25 mL of water into a graduated cylinder. She then placed an object in the cylinder. She now reads the volume as 42 mL. What is the volume of the object?

- ● 17 mL
- Ⓑ 25 mL
- Ⓒ 42 mL
- Ⓓ 67 mL

2 Four containers sit on a shelf. Which one contains a solution?

- Ⓕ the container with water in it
- Ⓖ the container with a rusty nail in it
- ● the container with lemonade in it
- Ⓘ the container with rocks and dirt in it

3 A golfer hits a golf ball so that it flies high into the air. What force brings the golf ball back to the ground?

- ● gravity
- Ⓑ friction
- Ⓒ magnetism
- Ⓓ atmospheric pressure

4 Two objects have the same volume. What measurement should you make to find out which object has the greater density?

- Ⓕ area
- ● mass
- Ⓗ length
- Ⓘ perimeter

---

5 Look at the illustration below.

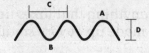

Which letter points to the crest of the wave?

- ● A
- Ⓑ B
- Ⓒ C
- Ⓓ D

6 A girl makes a cup of hot chocolate, but the hot chocolate is too hot. She places an ice cube in the cup. Which of the following **best** describes what happens when the hot chocolate comes in contact with the ice cube?

- Ⓕ The ice cube loses heat.
- Ⓖ The hot chocolate gains heat.
- ● The hot chocolate loses heat and the ice cube gains heat.
- Ⓘ The ice cube loses heat and the hot chocolate gains heat.

7 A man makes a noise in different locations. In which location will the sound from his noise travel the fastest?

- Ⓐ The sound will travel fastest down a long hallway.
- Ⓑ The sound will travel fastest through a pool of water.
- ● The sound will travel fastest through a solid metal rod.
- Ⓓ The sound will travel fastest from one side of a room to another.

---

8 Look at the illustration.
What is happening to the wood in this picture?

- Ⓕ It is undergoing a heat change from wood to ash.
- Ⓖ It is undergoing a phase change from wood to ash.
- Ⓗ It is undergoing a physical change from wood to ash.
- ● It is undergoing a chemical change from wood to ash.

9 When you use a doorknob to open a door, what simple machine are you using?

- Ⓐ lever
- Ⓑ pulley
- Ⓒ wedge
- ● wheel and axle

10 Four students make 4 different racing cars. To start the cars, each student pushes each car with the same amount of force. Which car will have the greatest speed?

- Ⓕ A 25 kilogram car moving across the grass.
- Ⓖ A 55 kilogram car moving across the grass.
- ● A 25 kilogram car moving along a paved road.
- Ⓘ A 55 kilogram car moving along a paved road.

11 A rider stands on a skateboard at the top of a hill. What happens when the rider starts to go down the hill?

- Ⓐ The skateboard's kinetic energy decreases.
- Ⓑ The skateboard's potential energy increases.
- ● The skateboard's potential energy changes to kinetic energy.
- Ⓓ The skateboard's kinetic energy changes to potential energy.

Write the answers to the questions on the lines.

12 Water can undergo physical changes when its temperature changes. Describe the types of physical changes water can undergo and explain what causes the changes. (2 points)

Water undergoes physical changes when it is heated or

cooled. Water that is heated changes from a liquid to a gas.

Water that is cooled (to freezing) changes from a liquid to a

solid. Solid water melts into a liquid when it warms.

13 Two students are using drums to make sound. Explain how the students are making sound and then explain how the students could make both soft and loud sounds. (2 points)

The students make sound when they tap on the drums. The

top of the drum vibrates and this makes a sound. One student

can make a soft sound by gently tapping. The other student

can make a loud sound with hard tapping on the drum.

Write your answer to the question on a separate sheet of paper.

14 Matter is all around us.

Part A Tell what matter is, what three forms it takes, and what it is made of.

Part B Tell the difference between an element and an atom. (4 points)

See page 188 for answer.

Unit C Test

Answer

⑭ *Part A* Matter is anything that takes up space and has weight. It can be a solid, liquid, or gas. Matter is made up of very small particles.

Part B An element is matter that is made up of a single type of particle. The smallest particle of an element that still has the properties of that element is called an atom.

Unit C Test Talk Answers

Strategy 1   page 90

1. I need to find out why astronauts exercise every day.
2. I need to find out what force helps you exercise on Earth.
3. I need to find out why astronauts don't feel the tug of gravity on the International Space Station.

Strategy 2   page 91

1. I found the answer in paragraph 3, sentence 2.
2. I found the answer in paragraph 2, sentence 1.
3. I found the answer in paragraph 2, sentence 6.

Strategy 3   page 92

1. C It helps keep bones and muscles healthy.
2. G gravity
3. B The high speed of the space station reduces gravity's effect.

Strategy 4   page 93

1. **My Notes:** gyms have machines based on those designed for space, people know more about keeping healthy
   My Answer: People on Earth have learned how to stay healthier from the information learned in space. Gyms also have equipment that is similar to the special machines made for exercising in space.
2. **My Notes:** machines similar to those on Earth: treadmill, bike, resistance machine
   My Answer: The machines used by astronauts are similar to the machines used on Earth. One is similar to a bicycle. Another is a type of treadmill. Astronauts also use rowing machines.

Strategy 5   page 94

1. To find the answer, I will look at the pictures and see how exercise equipment is different for astronauts than for people on Earth.
   My Answer: The astronauts are using similar machines, but there are straps on the machines so they do not float away.
2. To find the answer, I will look at the pictures and notice the different types of equipment the astronauts are using.
   My Answer: Accept all reasonable descriptions of the equipment pictured.

Strategy 6   page 95

1. To score higher, Mike needs to delete the information about gravity making exercise easier and replace it with a sentence about gravity making it harder to lift your arms and legs.
2. To score higher, Kay needs to explain why there is no gravity in space and why it is necessary to exercise. Kay needs to delete the sentence that says the machines are very different from machines on Earth since that is not accurate. She also should describe the exercise machines used by the astronauts.

Unit C Writing Prompt

Write a letter to explain what physical and chemical changes are to another student in your grade. Include an example of each type of change.

Grade 3 Writing Prompt Scoring Guide [Use with Unit C]

Score	Focus	Organization	Support	Conventions	Science Content
6	well focused on the topic	logical organizational pattern with a beginning, middle, and conclusion; excellent use of transitional devices	ample development of the supporting ideas, demonstrates a sense of completeness or wholeness; precision in word choice	generally correct subject/verb agreement and verb and noun forms; complete sentences except when fragments are used purposefully; a variety of sentence structures	no errors
5	focused on the topic	organizational pattern, with a few lapses; good use of transitional devices	adequate development of the supporting ideas with a sense of completeness or wholeness; adequate word choice but may lack precision	occasional errors in subject/verb agreement and in standard forms of verbs and nouns, but not enough to impede communication; generally follows conventions of punctuation, capitalization, and spelling; most sentences complete; some variety of sentence structures	few errors
4	fairly well focused on the topic but some loosely related information	evidence of an organizational pattern and transitional devices, but with some lapses	supporting ideas sometimes contain specifics and details but sometimes not developed; generally adequate word choice	demonstrates knowledge of conventions of punctuation and capitalization; correct spelling of commonly used words; an attempt to use a variety of sentence structures, although some are simple	some minor errors
3	generally focused on the topic but some extraneous information	organizational pattern attempted with some transitional devices, but some lapses	some supporting ideas not developed with specifics and details; adequate but limited word choice, occasionally vague	demonstrates knowledge of conventions of punctuation and capitalization, but some errors; correct spelling of commonly used words; an attempt to use a variety of sentence structures, although most are simple	1 or 2 significant errors
2	slightly related to topic	little evidence of an organizational pattern or transitional devices	development of supporting ideas often inadequate or illogical; limited or immature word choice	frequent errors in basic punctuation and capitalization; commonly used words frequently misspelled; primarily simple sentence constructions	significant errors
1	minimally addresses the topic	does not exhibit an organizational pattern	little, if any, development of supporting ideas, and usually provided through lists, clichés, and limited or immature word choice	frequent errors in spelling, capitalization, punctuation, and sentence structure; sentences primarily simple constructions	gross errors

Unscorable: The response has one or more of these problems: the response is not related to what the prompt requested the student to do; the response is simply a rewording of the prompt; the response is a copy of a published work; the student refused to write; the response is written in a foreign language; the response is illegible; the response is incomprehensible (words are arranged in such a way that no meaning is conveyed)

Anchor Paper: 6 points

Write a letter to explain what physical and chemical changes are to another student in your grade. Include an example of each type of change.

Dear James,

Have you ever cut wood and then burned it in a campfire? Those two activities show physical and chemical changes in matter. I will explain how.

Physical changes occur when matter changes the way it looks without becoming a new kind of matter. Tearing paper and cutting hair are physical changes. They generally cannot be undone. If you cut a piece of paper you cannot rejoin it. But both pieces are still paper.

Chemical changes occur when one kind of matter changes into another kind of matter. The Statue of Liberty looks green because the copper statue reacted with air and now has a layer of patina over it. Cookie batter baking into cookies is also a chemical change. Chemical changes cannot be reversed.

Remember my example of cutting wood and then burning it in a campfire? Cutting wood is a physical change because after it is cut the wood is still wood. Burning the wood in a fire is a chemical change because the wood becomes ash; it changes into new matter.

Let me know if you have any questions.

From,

Sarah

Score Point: 6

The writing focuses well on the topic. The organization has a beginning, middle, and conclusion with excellent use of transitional devices. The writing exhibits ample development of supporting ideas, demonstrates a sense of completeness or wholeness and a precision in word choice. Grammar usage is generally correct with subject/verb agreement and proper verb and noun forms. The paper is written in complete sentences except when fragments are used purposefully and there is variety in sentence structures. There are no errors in content.

Anchor Paper: 5 points

Write a letter to explain what physical and chemical changes are to another student in your grade. Include an example of each type of change.

Dear James,

Have you ever cut wood and then burned it in a campfire? Those two activities show physical and chemical changes in matter.

Physical changes happen when matter changes the way it looks without becoming a new kinds of matter. Tearing paper and cutting hair are physical changes. Physical changes generally cannot be undone.

Chemical changes happen when one kind of matter change into another kind of matter. Have you ever seen a rusty nail? That happens because the iron in the nail slowly changes to rust. This is a chemical change. Baking cookies is another type of chemical change.

Is cutting wood a physical or chemical change? It is a physical change because after it is cut the wood is still wood. Burning the wood in a fire is a chemical change because the wood becomes ash; the wood changes into new matter.

Let me know if you have any questions about physical and chemical changes.

From,

Sarah

Score Point: 5

The writing is focused on the topic. The paper is organized with only a few lapses and has good transitional devices. The writing is adequately developed, uses supporting ideas with a sense of completeness or wholeness. The word choice is adequate but may lack precision. There are occasional errors in subject/verb agreement and in standard forms of verbs and nouns, but not enough to impede communication. The conventions of punctuation, capitalization, and spelling are generally followed. Most sentences are complete and there is some variety of sentence structures. There are a few errors in content.

Anchor Paper: 4 points

Write a letter to explain what physical and chemical changes are to another student in your grade. Include an example of each type of change.

> Dear James,
>
> I wanted to write you a letter to explain how physical and chemical changes change matter.
>
> Physical changes are when matter changes the way it looks. The matter stays the same type of matter. Tearing paper and cutting vegetables into pieces are physical changes.
>
> Chemical changes are when one kind of matter change into another kind of matter. Rusting nails and eating food make chemical changes.
>
> Have you cut wood or burned wood? Cutting wood is a physical change. Burning the wood in a fire is a chemical change. One changes how wood looks. The other changes wood into new stuff, ash.
>
> Do you understand physical and chemical changes?
>
> From,
>
> Sarah

Score Point: 4

The writing focuses fairly well on the topic but contains some loosely related information. The paper shows evidence of an organizational pattern and transitional devices but has some lapses. The supporting ideas, while sometimes containing specifics and details, are sometimes also not developed. The word choice is generally adequate. The writing demonstrates knowledge of conventions of punctuation and capitalization and correct spelling of commonly used words. There is an attempt to use a variety of sentence structures, although some are simple. There are some minor errors in content.

Anchor Paper: 3 points

Write a letter to explain what physical and chemical changes are to another student in your grade. Include an example of each type of change.

Dear James,

Physical changes are when matter changes what it looks like, but not too much you can still tell what it is even after a physical change. Well, most of the time. Water turns to ice and that is a physical change and they don't look alike. Tearing paper and cutting wood into pieces are physical changes. Chemical changes are when one kind of matter change into another kind of matter. Rusting nials and eating food make chemical changes. Have you ever cut wood. Have you ever berned wood? One of them is a chemical change. Which one is it?

Sarah

Score Point: 3

The writing generally focuses on the topic but has some extraneous information. The paper shows an organizational pattern with some attempts to use transitional devices but some lapses occur. There are some supporting ideas but they are not developed with specifics and details. Word choice is adequate but limited and occasionally vague. The writing demonstrates knowledge of conventions of punctuation and capitalization but has some errors. Commonly used words are correctly spelled. An attempt is made to use a variety of sentence structures, although most are simple. There are 1 or 2 significant errors in content.

Anchor Paper: 2 points

Write a letter to explain what physical and chemical changes are to another student in your grade. Include an example of each type of change.

James,

Tering paper is a chemyical change. tering paper makes smaller peices of paper and The smaller peices is like.

Beking bred is a phsycial change. beking bread makes food. the bred is warm, the dogh is cold, the dogh is wet, the bred is dry?

Sarah

Score Point: 2

The writing is slightly related to the topic. There is little evidence of an organizational pattern or use of transitional devices. The development of supporting ideas is often inadequate or illogical. Word choice is limited or immature. The paper has frequent errors in basic punctuation and capitalization. Commonly used words are frequently misspelled. Sentence constructions are primarily simple. There are significant errors in content.

Anchor Paper: 1 point

Write a letter to explain what physical and chemical changes are to another student in your grade. Include an example of each type of change.

physical changes is when things changes the way it look benning would is physical change.

CHEMICAL changes is wehn a new thing are made and water turning to icee is chemical.

Every thing gots chemical and physical change. you no how would changes.

Sarah

Score Point: 1

The writing minimally addresses the topic and does not exhibit an organizational pattern. There are little, if any, supporting ideas and those ideas are usually provided through lists, clichés, and limited or immature word choice. The writing shows frequent errors in spelling, capitalization, punctuation, and sentence structure. Sentences are primarily simple constructions. There are gross errors in content.

© Pearson Education, Inc.

Unit C Performance Test Instructions

Investigating Physical Properties

Description: Students are asked to determine some physical properties of several objects by measuring their length, finding their mass, classifying them, describing their appearances, or testing their magnetism. They are asked to explain how they could make physical changes in the objects.

Purpose: To evaluate a student's ability to investigate objects in relation to their physical properties and investigate various ways that objects can undergo physical change.

Science Process Skill: Investigating

Time: Stations 1, 2, and 3 are designed to take students 40–45 minutes to complete.

Teacher Instructions

Station 1

Materials
> string (10 cm)
> string (15 cm)
> dental floss (20 cm)
> masking tape
> metric ruler
> Blackline Masters: pages 97 and 199

Preparation
1. Make copies of the blackline masters. Page 199 provides station setup instructions. Students can use page 97 to record their answers.
2. Use masking tape tags to label the 10 cm string "A" and the 15 cm string "B."
3. Use a masking tape tag to label the dental floss "C."

Teaching Tips
- Cotton string, made of several strands twisted together, is a good choice for this activity.
- You may want to tape the ends of the string and dental floss to prevent unraveling.
- Students can describe the strings using physical properties such as flexibility, length, and color.

Station 2

Materials

pan balance and set of masses
50 kidney beans
50 whole dried peas
50 lentils
paper plate
3 sealable bags labeled "A," "B," and "C"
Blackline Masters: pages 97 and 199

Preparation

1. Use page 199 to provide station setup instructions. Students can use page 97 to record their answers.

2. Find the mass of all the beans as well as the mass of each group of beans for your own information.

3. Place the beans and peas on a paper plate so they do not roll.

Teaching Tips

- Caution students not to eat any of the beans or peas.
- Students can classify the beans using physical properties such as size, shape, color, and mass.
- Monitor the station for dropped beans or peas.

Station 3

Materials

aluminum foil sheet (15 cm × 15 cm)
metal jar lid
aluminum can
4 paper clips
plastic bottle cap
magnet
Blackline Masters: pages 98 and 200

Preparation

1. Make copies of the blackline masters. Page 200 provides station setup instructions. Students can use page 98 to record their answers.

2. For your own reference, determine which objects are attracted to the magnet.

Teaching Tip

- Students can describe objects using physical properties such as color, shape, metal or nonmetal, and attraction to the magnet.

Station 1

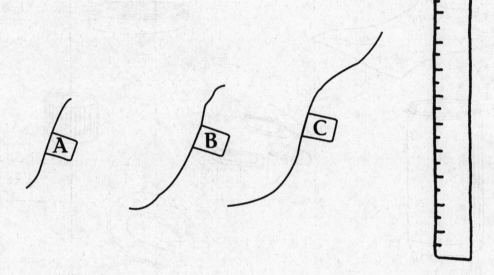

Be sure that the materials are set up like this before you leave this station.

Station 2

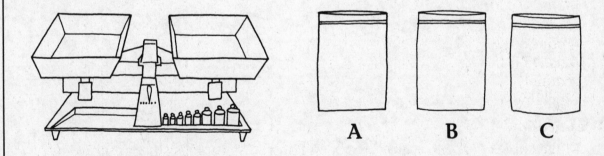

A   B   C

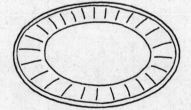

Be sure that the materials are set up like this before you leave this station.

Station 3

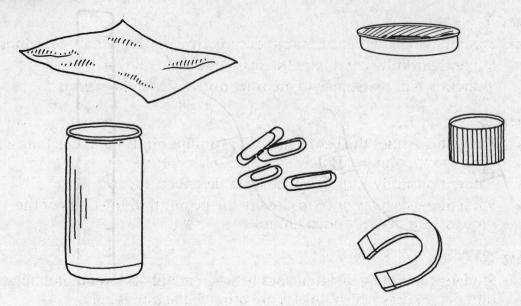

Be sure that the materials are set up like this before you leave this station.

Scoring Guide

Station 1

3 points   Student correctly measures and accurately describes the three strings.

2 points   Student partially completes the tasks described above.

1 point   Student needs assistance to measure and describe the strings.

Station 2

3 points   Student classifies the beans into three groups, finds the correct mass of each group, and accurately describes each group.

2 points   Student partially completes the tasks described above.

1 point   Student needs assistance to classify the beans, find the mass of the groups, and describe each group.

Station 3

3 points   Student accurately distinguishes between metal and nonmetal objects and determines which objects are attracted to a magnet.

2 points   Student accurately determines which objects are attracted to a magnet but does not distinguish between metal and nonmetal objects.

1 point   Student needs assistance to determine if an object is attracted to a magnet and if the object is metal or nonmetal.

Data Analysis

3 points   Student accurately describes a physical change for an item at each of the three stations.

2 points   Student accurately describes a physical change for an item at two of the three stations.

1 point   Student needs assistance to describe a physical change for any of the items at the three stations.

Total Score

Points	Percent equivalent
12	100
11	92
10	83
9	75
8	67
7	58
6	50
5	42
4	33
3	25
2	16
1	8

Investigating Physical Properties

Investigate the objects in the stations. Use their physical properties to describe them.

Station 1

Use the card at the station to correctly set up the equipment.

Strings

Record the lengths of the strings in the table. List three physical properties that describe each string.

String	Length	Description
A	10 cm	check students' responses
B	15 cm	check students' responses
C	20 cm	check students' responses

Station 2

Use the card at the station to correctly set up the equipment.

Beans

Classify the beans into three groups. Put the groups into the bags labeled "A," "B," or "C."

Record the mass of each bean group in the table. List three physical properties that describe each group.

Group	Mass	Description
A	check students' responses	check students' responses
B	check students' responses	check students' responses
C	check students' responses	check students' responses

Station 3

Use the card at the station to correctly set up the equipment.

Objects

Use the magnet to help investigate the objects. Divide the objects into two groups based on your investigation. Describe the two groups.

Group	Items	Description
1	check students' responses	check students' responses
2	check students' responses	check students' responses

Data Analysis

Now you have classified and measured all of the objects. Think about the physical properties of the items and use what you know to answer the following questions.

How could you make a physical change in the strings?

Possible answer: I could cut the string. This would make the string change size, but the string would still be a string.

How could you make a physical change in the beans?

Possible answer: I could soak a bean in water. This would make the bean change shape, but the bean would still be a bean.

How could you make a physical change in the paper clips?

Possible answer: I could bend a paper clip so it is straight instead of bent. This would make the paper clip change shape, but it would still be a paper clip.

Name _____

Read each question and choose the best answer. Then fill in the circle next to the correct answer.

1 Earth spins around an imaginary line called the
- ● axis.
- Ⓑ eclipse.
- Ⓒ horizon.
- Ⓓ rotation.

2 How long does it take for Earth to rotate one time?
- Ⓕ about 24 days
- Ⓖ about one year
- ● about 24 hours
- Ⓘ about one week

3 What causes shade beneath a tree?
- Ⓐ the seasons
- Ⓑ the phases of the Moon
- ● the tree blocking sunlight
- Ⓓ Earth reflecting sunlight

4 Shadows cast by the Sun are the shortest
- ● at noon.
- Ⓖ at night.
- Ⓗ in the morning.
- Ⓘ in the afternoon.

Assessment Book   Chapter 15 Test **99**

Name _____

5 The northern half of Earth tilts away from the Sun during which month below?
- Ⓐ June
- Ⓑ March
- ● December
- Ⓓ September

6 What causes the seasons to change on Earth?
- Ⓕ the tilt of Earth and its rotation
- Ⓖ the tilt of the Sun and its rotation
- ● the tilt of Earth and its revolution around the Sun
- Ⓘ the tilt of the Sun and its revolution around Earth

7 Complete the sentence.
In the summer, the number of hours of daylight is _____ the number of hours of darkness.
- Ⓐ less than
- Ⓑ the same as
- ● greater than
- Ⓓ about equal to

8 How long does it take the Moon to go once around Earth?
- Ⓕ longer than the four seasons put together
- Ⓖ longer than it takes Earth to go around the Sun
- Ⓗ about as long as it takes Earth to rotate once on its axis
- ● about as long as it takes the Moon to rotate once on its axis

100 Chapter 15 Test   Assessment Book

Name _____

9 Look at the illustration.

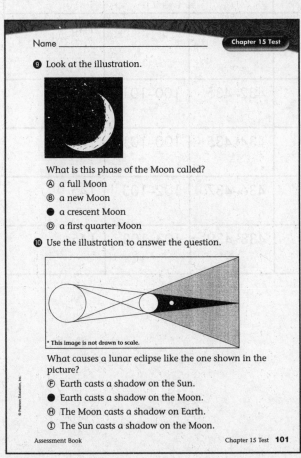

What is this phase of the Moon called?
- Ⓐ a full Moon
- Ⓑ a new Moon
- ● a crescent Moon
- Ⓓ a first quarter Moon

10 Use the illustration to answer the question.

* This image is not drawn to scale.

What causes a lunar eclipse like the one shown in the picture?
- Ⓕ Earth casts a shadow on the Sun.
- ● Earth casts a shadow on the Moon.
- Ⓗ The Moon casts a shadow on Earth.
- Ⓘ The Sun casts a shadow on the Moon.

Assessment Book   Chapter 15 Test **101**

Name _____

11 Why do some stars appear dimmer than others?
- Ⓐ They are bigger than other stars.
- Ⓑ They are hotter than other stars.
- Ⓒ They are closer to Earth than other stars.
- ● They are farther away from Earth than other stars.

Write the answers to the questions on the lines.

12 What would Earth be like without the Sun? (2 points)

Earth would be dark. Earth would be cold. Nothing would be

alive on Earth.

13 If you observe constellations at different times of the year, what will you notice about how they move? (2 points)

They are in different parts of the sky at different times of the

year. They seem to rotate around the North Star.

Write your answer to the question on a separate sheet of paper.

14 Explain why the full Moon is so bright at night even though it does not make light. Then tell how long it takes for the Moon to cycle from one full Moon to the next and what happens between full Moons. (4 points)
See page 204 for answer.

102 Chapter 15 Test   Assessment Book

Assessment Book   Answer Key **203**

Chapter 15 Test

Answer

⑭ The full Moon looks so bright at night because light from the Sun shines on the Moon and bounces off. It takes about 28 Earth days for the Moon to go from one full Moon to the next. In between full Moons the Moon goes through phases. We see less and less of the Moon each night until the new Moon when we can't see the Moon at all. Then we see more and more of the Moon each night until the next full Moon.

Intervention and Remediation

★ Science Objectives	Test Items	Student Edition Pages	Quick Study Pages	Workbook Pages
The student explains how the movement of the Earth in relation to the Sun determines the pattern of day and night.	1, 2	424–425	96–97	142
The student explains the patterns of change in shadows cast by the Sun in terms of the movement of Earth.	3, 4	426–427	96–97	142
The student knows that days and nights change in length throughout the year.	7, 12	428–431	98–99	143
The student knows the patterns of average temperatures throughout the year.	5, 6	430–431	98–99	143
The student explains how the Moon and Earth interact.	8, 10	432–435	100–101	144
The student knows the frequency of the lunar cycle is approximately 29 days.	9, 14	434–435	100–101	144
The student describes ways to study stars.	11	436–437	102–103	145
The student explains how constellations move.	13	438–439	102–103	145

Name _____

Read each question and choose the best answer.
Then fill in the circle next to the correct answer.

1 The Sun is
- ● a star.
- Ⓑ a comet.
- Ⓒ a planet.
- Ⓓ an asteroid.

2 Which of these planets is the farthest from the Sun?
- Ⓕ Venus
- Ⓖ Saturn
- Ⓗ Mercury
- ● Neptune

3 Why is Mercury very dry and hot?
- Ⓐ Mercury is the smallest planet.
- ● Mercury is the closest planet to the Sun.
- Ⓒ Mercury has a reddish surface that holds in the heat.
- Ⓓ Mercury has a thick atmosphere that holds in the heat.

4 A scientist describes a planet in this way: This planet is an inner planet with two moons. The planet has a reddish-orange rocky surface.
Which planet is the scientist describing?
- ● Mars
- Ⓖ Earth
- Ⓗ Venus
- Ⓘ Mercury

Name _____

5 Look at the illustration below.

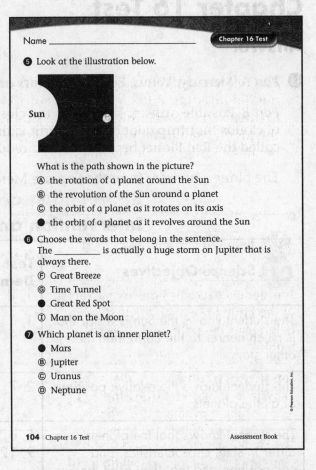

Sun

What is the path shown in the picture?
- Ⓐ the rotation of a planet around the Sun
- Ⓑ the revolution of the Sun around a planet
- Ⓒ the orbit of a planet as it rotates on its axis
- ● the orbit of a planet as it revolves around the Sun

6 Choose the words that belong in the sentence.
The _____ is actually a huge storm on Jupiter that is always there.
- Ⓕ Great Breeze
- Ⓖ Time Tunnel
- ● Great Red Spot
- Ⓘ Man on the Moon

7 Which planet is an inner planet?
- ● Mars
- Ⓑ Jupiter
- Ⓒ Uranus
- Ⓓ Neptune

Name _____

8 Look at the illustration below.

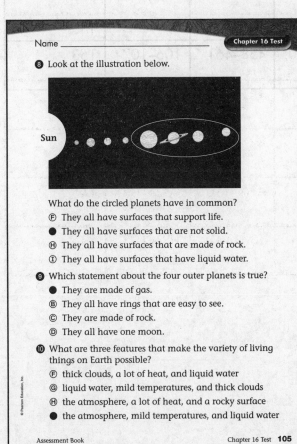

Sun

What do the circled planets have in common?
- Ⓕ They all have surfaces that support life.
- ● They all have surfaces that are not solid.
- Ⓗ They all have surfaces that are made of rock.
- Ⓘ They all have surfaces that have liquid water.

9 Which statement about the four outer planets is true?
- ● They are made of gas.
- Ⓑ They all have rings that are easy to see.
- Ⓒ They are made of rock.
- Ⓓ They all have one moon.

10 What are three features that make the variety of living things on Earth possible?
- Ⓕ thick clouds, a lot of heat, and liquid water
- Ⓖ liquid water, mild temperatures, and thick clouds
- Ⓗ the atmosphere, a lot of heat, and a rocky surface
- ● the atmosphere, mild temperatures, and liquid water

Name _____

Write the answers to the questions on the lines.

11 Explain why many stars look like pinpoints of light while the Sun seems very big and bright. (2 points)

The other stars in the sky look like pinpoints of light because

they are so far away. The Sun seems big and bright because it

is so close to Earth compared to the other stars.

12 Name the four outer planets and explain which one rotates different from the other three planets. (2 points)

Jupiter, Saturn, Uranus, and Neptune are the four outer

planets. Uranus orbits on its side.

_____

_____

Write your answer to the question on a separate sheet of paper.

13 The inner planets are closest to the Sun in our solar system.

Part A Name the four inner planets and describe a feature of each planet.

Part B List the order of the inner planets starting from the planet closest to the Sun.
(4 points)
        See page 206 for answer.

Chapter 16 Test

Answer

⑬ *Part A* Mercury, Venus, Earth, and Mars are the four inner planets.

Part B Possible answer: Mercury is the closest planet to the Sun. Venus has a thick layer of clouds that trap a lot of heat. Earth is the only planet that can support life. Mars is called the Red Planet because it has a reddish surface.

The planets in order from the Sun are Mercury, Venus, Earth, and Mars.

Intervention and Remediation

★ Science Objectives	Test Items	Student Edition Pages	Quick Study Pages	Workbook Pages
The student knows the Sun is a star that is much nearer to the Earth than the other stars.	1, 11	454–455	104–105	152
The student knows the relative positions of all the planets.	2, 7, 13	456–457	104–105	152
The student knows that the planets differ in size, characteristics, and composition and that they orbit the Sun in our solar system.	5, 6, 8, 9, 12	456–457, 462–465	104–107	152, 153
The student knows characteristics of Mercury, Venus, Earth, and Mars.	3, 4, 10, 13	458–461	106–107	153

**Read each question and choose the best answer.
Then fill in the circle next to the correct answer.**

1 Which answer **best** completes the sentence?
Technology is _____.
Ⓐ the study of computers
Ⓑ a science the Romans invented
Ⓒ asking a question about how the world works
● using knowledge to design a new way to do things

2 How do a heating system and an electrical system work together in a house?
Ⓕ The heating system turns the electrical system on and off.
● The electrical system turns the heating system on and off.
Ⓗ The heating system burns fuels to operate the electrical system.
Ⓘ The electrical system burns fuels to operate the heating system.

3 What invention did Percy Spencer develop after a chocolate bar melted in his pocket near a radar tube?
● the microwave oven
Ⓑ the convection oven
Ⓒ the drip coffee maker
Ⓓ the outdoor propane grill

---

4 Look at the illustration below.

Why are fibers, such as those you see in the picture, replacing standard wires in computer, telephone, and cable television systems?
Ⓕ The fibers shown do not get hot and can better scramble signals.
Ⓖ The fibers shown release more heat energy and can better scramble signals.
● The fibers shown do not get hot and can carry more information than standard wires can.
Ⓘ The fibers shown release more heat energy and can carry more information than standard wires can.

5 Which sentence is true about fuels used to generate electricity?
● The fuels can pollute the air.
Ⓑ The fuels were invented in Rome.
Ⓒ The fuels are renewable resources.
Ⓓ The fuels are called the greatest wonder of the world.

6 In the future, we may use which two renewable resources to meet our energy needs?
Ⓕ wind energy and coal
Ⓖ fossil fuels and natural gas
Ⓗ natural gas and solar energy
● wind energy and solar energy

---

7 In 312 B.C., Rome completed its first aqueducts. What did the aqueducts bring to Roman cities?
● water
Ⓑ electricity
Ⓒ medical care
Ⓓ safer food supplies

8 What two types of technology use a beam of light to read stored information?
● CDs and DVDs
Ⓖ VCR tapes and DVDs
Ⓗ audio cassettes and CDs
Ⓘ VCR tapes and audio cassettes

9 Look at the illustration below.

The panels on top of the house are using solar energy to make
Ⓐ fuel.
● hot water.
Ⓒ nuclear energy.
Ⓓ hydroelectric power.

10 What is a negative thing about wind and water power?
Ⓕ They are both renewable resources.
Ⓖ They are both nonrenewable resources.
Ⓗ They are both only available along a river.
● They both don't supply enough power for our needs.

Write the answers to the questions on the lines.

11 Identify two ways technology has changed the kitchen from the 1800s to today. (2 points)
Possible answer: In the 1800s kitchens had no electricity to keep things cold and fire was used to warm things up. Today, refrigerators use electricity to keep foods cold and microwave ovens cook food in minutes.

12 Why do some people call the National Highway System the greatest wonder of the modern world? (2 points)
Possible answer: The National Highway System is made of all the major highways that connect one state to another. The National Highway System carries supplies all over the nation and carries people throughout the country.

Write your answer to the question on a separate sheet of paper.

13 Water has been used for many years to generate power.
Part A Explain how water power is used in the modern age.
Part B Identify the positive and negative effects of using modern water power.
(4 points)
See page 208 for answer.

Chapter 17 Test

Answer

⑬ *Part A* In the modern age, dams are built to harness water power. Dams store the potential energy of water pressure and then release the water into the power station. This causes the blades of the water wheel in a generator to spin. This makes water energy change to electrical energy.

Part B Water power generates electricity that people need and it is a renewable energy source. However, dams can affect fish in rivers where dams are built. The large lake behind a dam floods the land, causing a change in the environment. Dams can also break and cause more flooding.

Intervention and Remediation

⭐ Science Objectives	Test Items	Student Edition Pages	Quick Study Pages	Workbook Pages
The student knows that, through the use of science processes and knowledge, people can solve problems, make decisions, and form new ideas.	1, 7	478–479	108–109	160
The student shows how a modern house consists of systems of parts.	2	480–481	108–109	160
The student understands that people invent new tools that affect life outside of science.	3, 4	484–485, 488–489	110–111	161
The student understands scientific discoveries have helped or hindered human health and lifestyles.	5, 8, 11, 12	482–483, 486–487, 493	108–109, 110–111, 112–113	160–162
The student evaluates the costs and benefits of using certain kinds of energy resources.	10, 13	490–495	112–113	162
The student knows that alternate energy sources are being explored.	6, 9	494–495	112–113	162

Read each question and choose the best answer.
Then fill in the circle next to the correct answer.

1 Why do stars look so small?
- ● They are very far away.
- Ⓑ They do not give off much light.
- Ⓒ They are all much smaller than our Sun.
- Ⓓ They are so crowded in space they can't take up much room.

2 Which of the following occurs about once every $29\frac{1}{2}$ days?
- ● a new Moon
- Ⓖ a solar eclipse
- Ⓗ a phase Moon
- Ⓘ a lunar eclipse

3 Choose the words that **best** complete the sentence.

Earth rotates on its _____ once every _____.
- ● axis, 24 hours
- Ⓑ axis, 365 days
- Ⓒ orbit, 24 hours
- Ⓓ orbit, 365 days

4 During the month of June, what position is Earth in?
- Ⓕ The South Pole points directly down.
- Ⓖ The South Pole points directly toward the Sun.
- ● The northern half of Earth tilts more toward the Sun.
- Ⓘ The northern half of Earth tilts more away from the Sun.

---

5 Look at the illustration below.

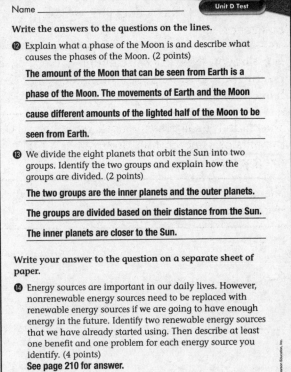

Which of these planets is an inner planet with a thick atmosphere and no moons?
- Ⓐ A
- ● B
- Ⓒ C
- Ⓓ D

6 Which of the following is true about the Sun?
- ● The Sun is a star that is the main source of energy for Earth.
- Ⓖ The Sun is a planet that is the main source of energy for Earth.
- Ⓗ The Sun is a star that provides a small amount of energy for Earth.
- Ⓘ The Sun is a planet that provides a small amount of energy for Earth.

7 A clue for a trivia game is: "This planet is a gas giant covered with thick layers of clouds. For years we've watched a huge storm on this planet and called it the Great Red Spot." What is the answer?
- Ⓐ Venus
- Ⓑ Saturn
- ● Jupiter
- Ⓓ Uranus

---

8 Look at the illustration below.

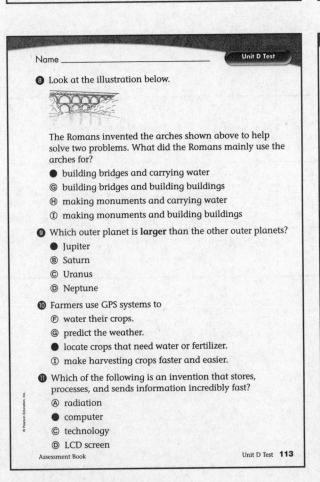

The Romans invented the arches shown above to help solve two problems. What did the Romans mainly use the arches for?
- ● building bridges and carrying water
- Ⓖ building bridges and building buildings
- Ⓗ making monuments and carrying water
- Ⓘ making monuments and building buildings

9 Which outer planet is **larger** than the other outer planets?
- ● Jupiter
- Ⓑ Saturn
- Ⓒ Uranus
- Ⓓ Neptune

10 Farmers use GPS systems to
- Ⓕ water their crops.
- Ⓖ predict the weather.
- ● locate crops that need water or fertilizer.
- Ⓘ make harvesting crops faster and easier.

11 Which of the following is an invention that stores, processes, and sends information incredibly fast?
- Ⓐ radiation
- ● computer
- Ⓒ technology
- Ⓓ LCD screen

Write the answers to the questions on the lines.

12 Explain what a phase of the Moon is and describe what causes the phases of the Moon. (2 points)

The amount of the Moon that can be seen from Earth is a

phase of the Moon. The movements of Earth and the Moon

cause different amounts of the lighted half of the Moon to be

seen from Earth.

13 We divide the eight planets that orbit the Sun into two groups. Identify the two groups and explain how the groups are divided. (2 points)

The two groups are the inner planets and the outer planets.

The groups are divided based on their distance from the Sun.

The inner planets are closer to the Sun.

Write your answer to the question on a separate sheet of paper.

14 Energy sources are important in our daily lives. However, nonrenewable energy sources need to be replaced with renewable energy sources if we are going to have enough energy in the future. Identify two renewable energy sources that we have already started using. Then describe at least one benefit and one problem for each energy source you identify. (4 points)
See page 210 for answer.

Unit D Test

Answer

⑭ Possible answer: Wind is a renewable energy source that we have already started using. Wind energy is beneficial because it does not cause pollution and since it is a renewable resource, it won't run out. One problem with wind energy is that the windmill blades must be huge.

Solar energy is another renewable energy source that we are beginning to use. Solar energy is beneficial because it does not cause pollution and it is a renewable resource. Some problems with solar energy include the cost of solar panels and the fact that the sun doesn't shine every day.

Unit D Test Talk Answers

Strategy 1   page 116

1. I need to find out the time it takes the Hubble Telescope to revolve around Earth.
2. I need to find out how often the Hubble Telescope sends information to Earth.
3. I need to find out why astronauts travel to the Hubble Telescope.

Strategy 2   page 117

1. I found the answer in paragraph 2, sentence 3.
2. I found the answer in paragraph 3, sentence 1.
3. I found the answer in paragraph 4, sentences 2, 3, and 4.

Strategy 3   page 118

1. C 97 minutes
2. F daily
3. C Astronauts put new technology on the Hubble Telescope.

Strategy 4   page 119

1. **My Notes:** replaced parts that have worn out, added new parts
   My Answer: Astronauts travel to the Hubble Telescope to replace parts that have worn out. They also travel to the telescope to add new parts so that it always has the newest technology.
2. **My Notes:** planets, black holes, quasars, star life
   My Answer: The Hubble Telescope collects information about planets such as Mars, Uranus, Pluto, and Neptune. The Hubble has also helped scientists learn about black holes, quasars, and star life cycles.

Strategy 5   page 120

1. To find the answer, I will look at the picture that shows the Hubble Telescope and study the telescope and think about what I know about energy sources.
   My Answer: The solar panels on the sides of the Hubble Telescope collect solar energy for the telescope to use in space.
2. To find the answer, I will look at the picture of the Hubble Telescope and compare that picture to what I know about other telescopes.
   My Answer: Accept all reasonable comparisons.

Strategy 6   page 121

1. To score higher, Ty needs to delete the information about collecting atmosphere samples since that is not accurate. He could also add information about the birth and death of stars.
2. To score higher, Jack needs to expand upon the sentence "It takes pictures..." because the Hubble actually takes more advanced pictures of objects than can be seen from Earth as well as objects that cannot be seen from Earth. Further, more detail can be added about Hubble's rotation and how often the Hubble sends data to Earth.

Unit D Writing Prompt

Your class is holding a debate about what energy sources scientists should develop for the future. Decide which renewable or nonrenewable resources you think should be developed for the future. Write an argument that explains why the resources you choose have more benefits than the other possibilities.

Grade 3 Writing Prompt Scoring Guide [Use with Unit D]

Score	Focus	Organization	Support	Conventions	Science Content
6	well focused on the topic	logical organizational pattern with a beginning, middle, and conclusion; excellent use of transitional devices	ample development of the supporting ideas, demonstrates a sense of completeness or wholeness; precision in word choice	generally correct subject/verb agreement and verb and noun forms; complete sentences except when fragments are used purposefully; a variety of sentence structures	no errors
5	focused on the topic	organizational pattern with a few lapses; good use of transitional devices	adequate development of the supporting ideas with a sense of completeness or wholeness; adequate word choice but may lack precision	occasional errors in subject/verb agreement and in standard forms of verbs and nouns, but not enough to impede communication; generally follows conventions of punctuation, capitalization, and spelling; most sentences complete; some variety of sentence structures	few errors
4	fairly well focused on the topic but some loosely related information	evidence of an organizational pattern and transitional devices, but with some lapses	supporting ideas contain details but sometimes not developed; generally adequate word choice	demonstrates knowledge of conventions of punctuation and capitalization; correct spelling of commonly used words; an attempt to use a variety of sentence structures, although some are simple	some minor errors
3	generally focused on the topic but some extraneous information	organizational pattern attempted with some transitional devices, but some lapses	some supporting ideas not developed with details; adequate but limited word choice; occasionally vague	demonstrates knowledge of conventions of punctuation and capitalization, but some errors; correct spelling of commonly used words; an attempt to use a variety of sentence structures, although most are simple	1 or 2 significant errors
2	slightly related to topic	little evidence of an organizational pattern or transitional devices	development of supporting ideas often inadequate or illogical; limited or immature word choice	frequent errors in basic punctuation and capitalization; commonly used words frequently misspelled; primarily simple sentence constructions	significant errors
1	minimally addresses the topic	does not exhibit an organizational pattern	little, if any, development of supporting ideas, and usually provided through lists, clichés, and limited or immature word choice	frequent errors in spelling, capitalization, punctuation, and sentence structure; sentences primarily simple constructions	gross errors

Unscorable: The response has one or more of these problems: the response is not related to what the prompt requested the student to do; the response is simply a rewording of the prompt; the response is a copy of a published work; the student refused to write; the response is written in a foreign language; the response is illegible; the response is incomprehensible (words are arranged in such a way that no meaning is conveyed)

Anchor Paper: 6 points

Your class is holding a debate about what energy sources scientists should develop for the future. Decide which renewable or nonrenewable resources you think should be developed for the future. Write an argument that explains why the resources you choose have more benefits than the other possibilities.

As scientists work toward developing energy sources for the future, they should focus on renewable resources, such as solar power and wind power. Solar power and wind power have many advantages over various types of nonrenewable resources.

Solar power and wind power are both natural renewable resources, which means that the supply will never run out. Nonrenewable resources, such as coal or petroleum, have a limited supply and will eventually run out. Some natural renewable resources, such as wood, are replaceable.

Solar power and wind power also do not generate air pollution. Burning nonrenewable fossil fuels creates a lot of air pollution. Also, mining for the fossil fuels can cause land and water pollution. Burning a natural renewable resource, like wood, also creates pollution.

Lastly, solar power and wind power are becoming more affordable while nonrenewable fossil fuel costs are becoming more expensive. If scientists work to develop better equipment to collect the energy of the Sun and wind, affordable, renewable energy sources could be available to all.

Score Point: 6

The writing focuses well on the topic. The organization has a beginning, middle, and conclusion with excellent use of transitional devices. The writing exhibits ample development of supporting ideas, demonstrates a sense of completeness or wholeness and a precision in word choice. Grammar usage is generally correct with subject/verb agreement and proper verb and noun forms. The paper is written in complete sentences except when fragments are used purposefully and there is variety in sentence structures. There are no errors in content.

Grade 3

Anchor Paper: 5 points

Your class is holding a debate about what energy sources scientists should develop for the future. Decide which renewable or nonrenewable resources you think should be developed for the future. Write an argument that explains why the resources you choose have more benefits than the other possibilities.

As scientists work toward developing energy sources for the future, they should focus on renewable resources, such as solar power and wind power. Solar power and wind power have many advantages over various types of nonrenewable resources.

Solar power and wind power are both natural renewable resources, which means that the supply will never run out. Other nonrenewable resources, such as coal or petroleum, have a limited supply and will eventually run out.

Solar power and wind power also do not make any pollution. Burning fossil fuels creates a lot of air pollution. Also, mining for the fossil fuels can cause other kinds of pollution. Burning natural a renewable resource, like wood, also creates pollution.

Lastly, solar power and wind power are very expensive, just like fossil fuels. However, if scientists work to develop better equipment using renewable resources will be affordable for everyone.

Score Point: 5

The writing is focused on the topic. The paper is organized with only a few lapses and has good transitional devices. The writing is adequately developed, uses supporting ideas with a sense of completeness or wholeness. The word choice is adequate but may lack precision. There are occasional errors in subject/verb agreement and in standard forms of verbs and nouns, but not enough to impede communication. The conventions of punctuation, capitalization, and spelling are generally followed. Most sentences are complete and there is some variety of sentence structures. There are a few errors in content.

Grade 3

Anchor Paper: 4 points

Your class is holding a debate about what energy sources scientists should develop for the future. Decide which renewable or nonrenewable resources you think should be developed for the future. Write an argument that explains why the resources you choose have more benefits than the other possibilities.

Scientists should develop renewable resources, like solar power and wind power. Solar power and wind power are better than nonrenewable resources for a lot of reasons.

Solar power and wind power are both natural renewable resources so the supply will never run out. Fossil fuels have a limited supply and will eventually run out. That's why you don't want to use them.

Solar power and wind power also do not make any pollution. Burning fossil fuels creates a lot of air pollution. Natural resources are better than nonrenewable resources because they don't make pollution.

Solar power and wind power can make a lot of energy. They can make enough energy for the whole Earth. Fossil fuels can't. Fossil fuels also cost a lot of money. Gas keeps getting more expensive. The Sun's energy is free. So is the winds.

Score Point: 4

The writing focuses fairly well on the topic but contains some loosely related information. The paper shows evidence of an organizational pattern and transitional devices but has some lapses. The supporting ideas, while sometimes containing specifics and details, are sometimes also not developed. The word choice is generally adequate. The writing demonstrates knowledge of conventions of punctuation and capitalization and correct spelling of commonly used words. There is an attempt to use a variety of sentence structures, although some are simple. There are some minor errors in content.

Grade 3

Your class is holding a debate about what energy sources scientists should develop for the future. Decide which renewable or nonrenewable resources you think should be developed for the future. Write an argument that explains why the resources you choose have more benefits than the other possibilities.

Scientists should work on nonrenewable resources, like soler power and wind power. Soler power and wind power are better than renewable resources for a lot of reasons.

Soler power and wind power are both nonrenewable resources so the supply will never run out. Fossil fuels can run out, so we should stop using them before they run out. Oil and gas are going to run out soon. There is a lot of petroleum and coal still buried. We just need to find it.

Soler power and wind power are clean. Fossil fuels are dirty. Fossil fuels make the air dirty. They make it hard for people to breathe. Lots of dirty air is smoge. We dont' want smoge.

Soler power makes a lot of power. Wind power makes a lot of power. With a lot of power, a lot of things can work. Can you imagin a soler car? Or a wind car? That is what scientists should make.

Score Point: 3

The writing generally focuses on the topic but has some extraneous information. The paper shows an organizational pattern with some attempts to use transitional devices but some lapses occur. There are some supporting ideas but they are not developed with specifics and details. Word choice is adequate but limited and occasionally vague. The writing demonstrates knowledge of conventions of punctuation and capitalization but has some errors. Commonly used words are correctly spelled. An attempt is made to use a variety of sentence structures, although most are simple. There are 1 or 2 significant errors in content.

Grade 3

Anchor Paper: 2 points

Your class is holding a debate about what energy sources scientists should develop for the future. Decide which renewable or nonrenewable resources you think should be developed for the future. Write an argument that explains why the resources you choose have more benefits than the other possibilities.

> Soler is better than renewable resources.
>
> Soler power is a non re new able resource. They're supply can run out. Gas is going to run out too. that is why costts alot Soler power costts alot to. that is why noone has it.
>
> Soler power is outside. It can only be used outside. Cars shood use soler power cars use gas and make things dirty.

Score Point: 2

The writing is slightly related to the topic. There is little evidence of an organizational pattern or use of transitional devices. The development of supporting ideas is often inadequate or illogical. Word choice is limited or immature. The paper has frequent errors in basic punctuation and capitalization. Commonly used words are frequently misspelled. Sentence constructions are primarily simple. There are significant errors in content.

Grade 3

Anchor Paper: 1 point

Your class is holding a debate about what energy sources scientists should develop for the future. Decide which renewable or nonrenewable resources you think should be developed for the future. Write an argument that explains why the resources you choose have more benefits than the other possibilities.

> gas shood bee used by scyentysts because there is alot of it underground and noone is using it for anything besides cars and there are alot of cars by they dont' use alot off gas.
>
> gas is good because it is easy to find at gas stashuns and placs like that you can put it in gugs and carry it with you. then you always heve enrgy.

Score Point: 1

The writing minimally addresses the topic and does not exhibit an organizational pattern. There are little, if any, supporting ideas and those ideas are usually provided through lists, clichés, and limited or immature word choice. The writing shows frequent errors in spelling, capitalization, punctuation, and sentence structure. Sentences are primarily simple constructions. There are gross errors in content.

Unit D Performance Test Instructions
Using a Model to Investigate the Moon's Appearance

Description: Students are asked to make models of a new moon, a first quarter moon, and a lunar eclipse. They are asked to describe how the positions of the Sun, Moon, and Earth affect the appearance of the Moon.

Purpose: To evaluate a student's ability to use a model to illustrate an understanding of the positions of the Sun, Earth, and Earth's moon during phases of the Moon and lunar eclipses.

Science Process Skill: Using a Model

Time: Stations 1, 2, and 3 are designed to take students 40–45 minutes to complete.

Teacher Instructions

Station 1
Materials

    modeling clay
    plastic bag
    pencil
    flashlight
    Blackline Masters: pages 123 and 221

Preparation

1. Make copies of the blackline masters. Page 221 provides station setup instructions. Students can use page 123 to record their answers.
2. Place the modeling clay in a plastic bag to keep it from drying out.

Teaching Tips

- If a flashlight is unavailable, you can use a small table lamp instead. Be sure to remind students to be careful working around the cord.
- You may need to darken the room for students to make accurate observations.
- Students should recognize that by holding the model between the flashlight and themselves, the new moon is modeled.

Station 2
Materials
> modeling clay
> plastic bag
> pencil
> flashlight
> Blackline Masters: pages 123 and 221

Preparation
1. Use page 221 to provide station setup instructions. Students can use page 123 to record their answers.
2. Place the modeling clay in a plastic bag to keep it from drying out.

Teaching Tips
- If a flashlight is unavailable, you can use a small table lamp instead. Be sure to remind students to be careful working around the cord.
- You may need to darken the room for students to make accurate observations.
- Students should recognize that by holding the ball out with their right arm into the path of the flashlight, the first quarter Moon is modeled.

Station 3
Materials
> modeling clay
> plastic bag
> pencil
> flashlight
> Blackline Masters: pages 124 and 222

Preparation
1. Make copies of the blackline masters. Page 222 provides station setup instructions. Students can use page 124 to record their answers.
2. Divide the modeling clay into a small piece and a large piece. Place the modeling clay in a plastic bag to keep it from drying out.

Teaching Tips
- Students should be sure that they create a model of the appearance of the Moon during a full Moon phase before placing the model of Earth into the eclipse model.
- If a flashlight is unavailable, you can use a small table lamp instead. Be sure to remind students to be careful working around the cord.
- You may need to darken the room for students to make accurate observations.
- Students should recognize that by placing the model of Earth between the flashlight and the Moon model, they model a lunar eclipse.

Station 1

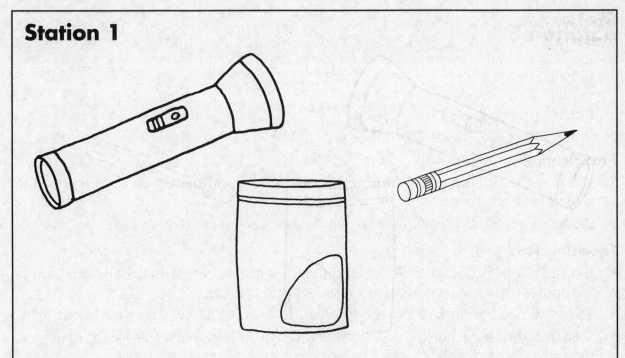

Be sure that the materials are set up like this before you leave this station.

Station 2

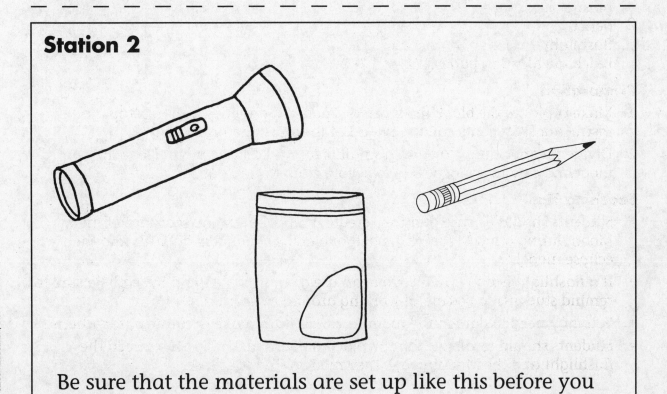

Be sure that the materials are set up like this before you leave this station.

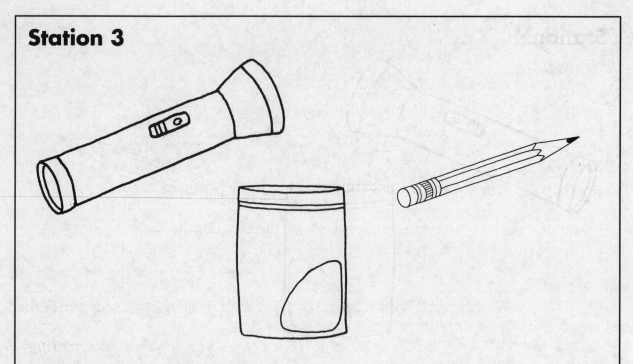

Be sure that the materials are set up like this before you leave this station.

Scoring Guide

Station 1

3 points   Student correctly models and identifies the phase of the new Moon.

2 points   Student correctly models the phase but misidentifies it.

1 point   Student needs assistance to perform both tasks.

Station 2

3 points   Student correctly models and identifies the phase of the first quarter Moon.

2 points   Student correctly models the phase but misidentifies it.

1 point   Student needs assistance to perform both tasks.

Station 3

3 points   Student correctly draws the model of the lunar eclipse and identifies the eclipse as a lunar eclipse.

2 points   Student correctly draws the model of the lunar eclipse but misidentifies the type of eclipse.

1 point   Student needs assistance to perform both tasks.

Data Analysis

3 points   Student accurately describes how the appearance of the Moon depends on the positions of the Sun, Earth, and Moon.

2 points   Student describes how the appearance of the Moon depends on the positions of the Sun, Earth, and Moon, with fewer than two errors.

1 point   Student needs assistance providing the description.

Total Score

Points	Percent equivalent
12	100
11	92
10	83
9	75
8	67
7	58
6	50
5	42
4	33
3	25
2	16
1	8

Modeling the Moon's Appearance

Imagine that you must model the phases of the Moon and a lunar eclipse for a class presentation. Your job is to correctly show the appearance of the Moon using a model.

Station 1

Use the card at the station to correctly set up the equipment.

Moon Phases I

Make a clay ball and put it on the end of the pencil. Place the flashlight on a table and turn it on. Hold the ball halfway between you and the light. Observe how much of the part of the ball you can see is lighted. Name the phase of the Moon you modeled.

New Moon _____

Station 2

Use the card at the station to correctly set up the equipment.

Moon Phases II

Make a clay ball and put it on the end of the pencil. Place the flashlight on a table and turn it on. Hold the ball out with your right arm into the path of the light. Turn your head. Observe how much of the ball you can see is lighted. Name the phase of the Moon you modeled.

First Quarter Moon _____

Station 3

Use the card at the station to correctly set up the equipment.

Eclipse

Shape the clay into a model of the Moon and place it on the pencil. Shape a model of Earth using a larger piece of clay. Set the flashlight on one side of a table and set the model of the Moon on the other side of the table. Hold the model of Earth midway between the Moon model and the flashlight. Observe how Earth affects the appearance of the Moon.

Draw a picture of the appearance of the Moon in your model and name the type of eclipse you modeled.

> **Check students' drawings of a lunar eclipse.**

Lunar Eclipse _____

Data Analysis

How do the positions of the Sun, Moon, and Earth affect the appearance of the Moon?

Possible answer: Since the Moon reflects light from the Sun, the appearance of the Moon depends on how the Sun strikes it as well as where the Moon is in its orbit around Earth. As the Moon orbits around Earth, its appearance changes. Sometimes, when Earth is between the Sun and Moon a lunar eclipse occurs because Earth's shadow falls over the Moon.